ASHLEY BERRY

Waiting for Rainbows

AN AUTOBIOGRAPHY

TSPA THE SELF PUBLISHING AGENCY

Ashley Berry

Waiting for Rainbows

TSPA The Self Publishing Agency

Copyright © 2021 by Ashley Berry

First Edition

Softcover ISBN: 978-1-954233-11-9
Electronic ISBN: 978-1-954233-12-6

Cover Design | Stephanie MacDougall
Book Layout | Kristy Twellmann Hill

Editors | Alison Whyte & Elise Volkman

Author Photo | Kassie George Photography

Publishing Support | TSPA The Self Publishing Agency

Disclaimer

Though this book covers some medical details surrounding infertility and PCOS, the contents are not intended to be a substitute for professional medical advice, diagnosis, or treatment. Always seek the advice of your physician or other qualified health provider regarding a medical condition.

Some names and identifying details have been changed to protect the privacy of individuals.

Dedicated to

my two rainbows,
Mox and Mya

TABLE OF CONTENTS

PREFACE

I WANTED TO GIVE UP SO MANY TIMES DURING our journey to our family, but I kept picking myself up and moving forward. I knew that I was going to be a mom. I didn't know how or when; I just knew I had to keep the faith, keep fighting, and keep pushing on.

I hope this book will inspire you as you read it. You may be going through infertility or the journey to adoption. It may seem like your dream will never happen. I want to share our story to help you during the times that feel hopeless. I hope it will give you that drive to keep trying. Sometimes we can get so set on one way of thinking that we miss out on things in life that we could have tried—things that we weren't expecting.

For those of you reading because you want to support someone who has been going through something similar, our story may help you to understand a little more of what they may be feeling or experiencing. I hope you find the words and understanding you need to try to help them through it. Thank you for offering them your support and loving them through their journey.

And maybe you're not reading this for any of these reasons. Maybe life is throwing hoops and hurdles at you in some other way. I hope this book gives you the drive to keep going, to keep fighting, and to keep hoping for your rainbow.

Live in hope,

Ashley

MEETING CAL

July 2007 – October 2008

IT WAS THE SUMMER OF 2007, AND SHAYLA and I were bored.

We had been spending a lot of time together that summer. I met Shayla while working with her at the Holiday Inn. She was spontaneous and fun; we became fast friends. I was in my third year of college as an Art Major, specializing in photography. I took pictures of anything and everything anyway, so I'd decided to try to make a career out of it.

It was July 3rd, we had nothing going on, and Shayla's ex was just across the way at a friend's place. He and Shayla had been in a serious relationship in high school and though they were no longer together, they texted back and forth sometimes.

She happened to be texting with him that night. It turned out we were all looking for something to do. Shayla told him we were having some people over. She told him to come and bring his friends. Call it impulsive, spur of the moment, whatever—it really was only us two, but we didn't want to sound desperate for company.

Before they came, Shayla set down some ground rules.

"I know all these guys," she said, "and the only one you should talk to is Cal."

Apparently, he was one of the good ones. I didn't really think anything of it until I happened to look out the window and saw fifteen guys coming across the street.

I looked at Shayla. "Oh my goodness, Shayla. We're having a party?"

She laughed at me, we turned up the music, and the beer pong began.

I loved the place that I lived in at the time. It was an older house with so much character. The outside walls were painted peach, and it had an open floor plan from the dining room to the living room. It was big enough for me to put in a pool table with a ping pong attachment.

I lived on the main floor and I didn't have an air conditioner, so it was very hot. We had the windows open to let in the outside air, and before long we were having a great time. I had won quite a few games of beer pong and was feeling pretty proud of myself when I finally decided to take a break. That's when I started to chat with one of the guys.

I didn't even introduce myself at first. I don't really remember what we talked about, but after about ten minutes I finally said to him, "What's your name?"

"I'm Cal," he said.

"Oh, *you're* Cal!" I smiled. "I can talk to *you*."

Half an hour later, we were kissing in the kitchen. I guess that's what you'd call instant sparks!

I didn't take any pictures of that night, but I'll never forget what I was wearing, because that was the night I met Cal. I still own the black tank top and jean skirt that I wore that day.

Three days later, Cal was picking me up for our first date. We went to see the new *Transformers* movie. Shayla had played Miss Matchmaker—and played her well. Cal and I started to spend a lot more time together and our relationship moved quickly after that. I started working at a local photography studio while I finished my degree. I did sessions and helped with the editing. The owner didn't do weddings, so I started up my own little wedding photography business through her as well.

On the side, I started helping Cal with his job. He worked for his Uncle Jerry and Aunt June at their family-owned greenhouse. Cal and his sister Breanna also had a very large garden. They sold produce and cut flowers at a local farmer's market. He would normally come over after he was done working, and he would be pretty tired every night. I could tell he was a hard worker. His job was very physical and draining.

I also found out that I wasn't the only girl in Cal's life. I met Skeeter early on, his fifty-pound German Shorthaired Pointer. I'm pretty sure Skeeter lived every dog's dream. She ran free on forty acres of land and went to the greenhouse every day with Cal. Aunt June made sure to drop a treat for her every hour.

After Cal and I had dated for about a year, we decided to move in together. Skeeter got used to sleeping with us and one night I guess she decided to remind me that she came first. I was in a deep sleep and she let one go. I woke up to the most horrendous smell, opened my eyes, and found her butt right there in my face.

Ewwww!

That wasn't the only lesson I had to learn, either. When I first started joining Cal at the greenhouse, everything was so new to me. I didn't know the difference between perennial and annual plants. The first time he asked me to trim the million bells, my response was, "Won't that kill them?"

He might have looked at me a little funny. "It'll make them more full and uniform," he told me. It was only the first of many lessons. I knew that if I wanted this to last, I was going to have to learn to love dirt, plants, and learning. And Skeeter.

Cal's grandfather had started the greenhouse and kept it small until Uncle Jerry took over and expanded. He added a bigger greenhouse and Cal started learning from him when he was in the eighth grade. Cal knew early on what he wanted to do for his career, and Uncle Jerry quickly became like a second father to him.

October 13th, 2008 was a regular, old Monday. Cal and I had been seeing each other for sixteen months, and I was getting used to helping at the greenhouse and managing the rest of my schedule at that point. That day, I got home from work at the studio and Cal's truck was already there. I was surprised he beat me home. His work at the greenhouse wasn't only physically demanding; it demanded a lot of his time as well. I was usually home before he was.

I walked into the house and he already had supper made. I'm sure he was tired from a busy day of picking—Monday was always a picking day—but he had showered and was wearing a nice button-down shirt.

"Wow, you made supper! Looks great!" I said.

I had no idea what had gotten into him. I sat down and we ate, but I felt like he was nervous about something the whole time. And that made *me* nervous. It was a great supper—everything tasted good and he had put in all that work after a long day—but I was having a hard time eating. I couldn't shake the thought that something was about to happen.

After we finished, I sat down on the couch. Cal didn't. He got down on one knee in front of me and opened a black box.

Oh my goodness! Is this happening?

"Will you marry me?" he asked.

I said, "YES!" and hugged him tight.

The beautiful ring Cal gave me has one square diamond in the middle with smaller ones along the band. I loved it then, and I still love it now.

After we'd both calmed down a bit, he told me that when he walked out of the bathroom after he'd showered, he caught Skeeter up on the table eating our salad. I'm not sure she was as happy about the engagement as we were, but I was so excited! I couldn't wait to start planning. The main thought that ran through my head in all the excitement was:

I can't wait to start our family!

TRYING

September 2009 – September 2012

I WAS READY TO START TRYING FOR OUR family a few months after our wedding. But Cal wasn't.

I knew he had good reasons for wanting to wait. We were going to be busy for nine months straight every year. Greenhouse season ran from March to June, vegetable season ran from July to September, and Cal wanted to start up a pumpkin patch and a corn maze in the fall. We both liked moving fast and keeping busy.

But I knew we were always going to be busy. Cal was still working for Jerry as an hourly employee, hoping one day he would be able to take over the greenhouse. Life wasn't going to slow down for us anytime soon, and if we wanted a family, we would have to adapt or change some things to make it work.

I also knew that we had to be on the same page with this decision. I talked with Cal and tried to convince him, and then I talked to him some more.

"What about all the work?"

"How are we going to take care of kids when we're so busy?"

"Where are we even gonna put them?"

Cal had lots of fair questions and there were details to work out; I knew it wouldn't happen right away. I was happy just to be living life with him. But I wanted this—I wanted our family to grow—so I kept talking with him about it.

And nine months after our wedding, we decided to start trying.

I didn't get my hopes up that it would happen right away. We may have moved quickly in our relationship, but I knew this could take time. I knew it could take a while and I was willing to wait.

The months went by and still, the two pink lines failed to appear. After about six months of trying, each month started to get harder and harder. Knowing that I wasn't getting pregnant weighed on me. I became convinced that something must be wrong. I had mentioned to my doctor at a yearly checkup that we were trying, and she told me that if nothing happened for a year, then we should start seeking medical help.

In the spring of 2011, that year mark came. We had been trying for twelve whole months. But doctors' appointments would have to wait for a few months more because our city was about to go through some major trauma.

The greenhouse is built right beside a river, and that year the river flooded. The water made it about halfway up the greenhouse walls. The house we rented from Cal's mom Lynn filled with water up to the roof. The new store we had built for the pumpkin patch and corn maze was full of water up to the windows, and all the pumpkins and produce were under water. There was so much loss for so many people that year. We had no idea how much more loss was yet to come.

We had to find another place to live right away, but the market was tough. We hadn't intended to buy yet. The plan was always to rent from Cal's mom until we could build our own place close to the greenhouse. We had to adapt again.

When we contacted the realtor, our only option was a townhouse at the south end of town, but it wouldn't be ready for us right away. We needed a place to stay in the meantime. Luckily, Cal's sister's house hadn't flooded, so Breanna invited us to stay with her and her husband.

While we were staying there, our doctor recommended I start a round of medication called Clomid to increase the amount of hormones that support the growth and release of a mature egg.

My first appointment was an ultrasound on day three of my cycle. They had to check my follicles to make sure I could start the medication. The ultrasound results came back normal, so I started with the Clomid pills. I had another ultrasound to time everything out so they'd know when I would be ovulating. Then we had to wait two weeks to take a pregnancy test and find out if everything worked.

It wasn't successful. I was disappointed, but since we'd been trying for over a year, it didn't really surprise me that it didn't work.

Next, they wanted me to do a hystersalpingogram (HSG) test to check my Fallopian tubes. For the HSG test, they insert a balloon to open up your cervix and run dye through your tubes to make sure there's no blockage. When I showed up for my appointment, the doctor warned me the procedure wouldn't feel very good.

"You'll start cramping pretty bad."

He wasn't kidding. As soon as he started, the pain was so intense I thought I was going to throw up.

He asked me how I was doing.

I answered between clenched teeth. "I'm okay."

"Wow, you're doing great. You're tough!"

If only he knew how I really felt.

When I looked at the screen during that appointment, my Fallopian tubes looked *so* tiny, like little strings. Were they supposed to look like that?

The test results came back normal, but we still had no luck. We had to skip the next cycle. They said I couldn't do another Clomid cycle yet due to cysts that had developed on my ovaries. I would have to do another ultrasound on day three of my next cycle to see if we could proceed with that one.

We were still living at Breanna's house while all of this was happening, and one day she announced that they were pregnant. I was so happy for them, but living with them while Cal and I were at the height of our infertility—seeing her growing bump, the maternity and baby clothes, watching her prepare a nursery—was *a lot* for me at the time.

I did not like the person infertility was turning me into. I started to become distant from everything, like I was trying to protect myself from feeling hurt or having feelings I didn't like. I've always been a very positive person, but this experience was turning me into a negative person; it was someone I didn't want to be.

Cal didn't show many feelings about not getting pregnant. It didn't seem to bother him as much. But, since he wasn't the one actually trying to get pregnant, I think it was hard for him to understand what I was going through.

I felt like everyone around me was getting pregnant, moving forward with their lives, and growing their families. It seemed so easy and natural for them. We were trying everything, and it wasn't happening. I felt trapped—stuck—like we were in a strange state of limbo, or a cycle of groundhog days that would never end.

But it was time to move on to the next step and I was ready for something to change. An in vitro fertilization (IVF) doctor came to our clinic once a month to see new patients and we booked an appointment with him. He looked over all the previous ultrasounds I had gone through, and at our appointment he started to ask me some questions.

"Do you have excessive body hair?"

"Yep."

"Do you suffer from acne? Infertility? Easy weight gain?"

"Yep, yep, yep."

"Irregular cycles?"

That was the only question that changed my answer. "No, my cycles are normally right on time: twenty-eight days."

It was all he needed to know to give me an answer, for a change.

"You have PCOS—polycystic ovarian syndrome. You don't have all of the symptoms, but you have the majority. Your previous ultrasounds show that you also had cycles where there were a lot of tiny cysts on your ovaries."

That was true. I remembered seeing them. They'd looked like a string of pearls on the ultrasound.

"That confirmed my diagnosis," the doctor said.

He also explained that many women manage to get pregnant even though they have PCOS, and he gave us our next step: I would start on Metformin medication, which would hopefully ease my symptoms and help my body produce healthy, mature eggs.

After that appointment I felt some relief. I finally had some answers after so many months of questions. But I felt defeated at the same time. More tests and more complications—this wasn't helping the person I was becoming.

We decided to try an intrauterine insemination (IUI) cycle. It's one of the first treatments doctors recommend to help couples with getting pregnant, or to treat unexplained infertility. IUI starts with an ultrasound at the beginning of each cycle to make sure everything is working properly before moving forward with the process. After the ultrasound, you are given a medication that stimulates your ovaries to mature the eggs. Timing is very important. The doctors want to know when your eggs are ready and when you are about to ovulate. The IUI procedure needs to be done a day or two after ovulation, so as ovulation gets closer, you have to have ultrasounds every other day in order to know when everything is ready.

Before any of that, though, our IVF doctor said he also wanted me to do another HSG.

"The last time I had that done I almost threw up!" I told him. I had no desire to go through that again.

But he told me that the doctor who would be doing my IUI was the same one who would perform the HSG, and he was great.

Here we go again.

At this next HSG test, while I was laying down and bracing myself for the pain, the doctor chatted with me. He asked me questions and made conversation. I don't remember what we talked about, but I was still bracing myself for the pain when he looked at me and said, "All done."

"What? That didn't hurt at all! It went so fast."

I told him the first time I had the procedure done it hurt so much I almost threw up. Our IVF doctor was right. He *was* good. I couldn't help feeling a bit more hopeful knowing that he would be the one to start us on IUI.

Between appointments and helping with work at the greenhouse, I tried to do some research on PCOS, so I could educate myself. I wanted to do whatever I could do to produce good eggs and hopefully have a successful pregnancy, but there wasn't a lot of information out there at that time.

By the time we were ready to start the IUI process, I was excited to move forward. I had such high hopes that it was going to work. I had another ultrasound at the beginning of my cycle and, once I got the go ahead, I started medication to help me produce some nice, mature eggs. As I got close to ovulation, I had an ultrasound every other day so that we would know when the follicles were ready. Then, I gave myself an Ovidrel shot to stimulate ovulation. Cal gave his sample, which was then washed and placed in a catheter, and that was placed in my uterus so it could meet my egg without having to go through any hoops or hurdles.

The procedure was fast and painless. It was what came after that was the hard part: the two-week wait to see if it worked.

That was one of the longest two weeks of my life. I tried to distract myself with work and other things in my schedule, but it wasn't something I could just push out of my mind. The twisted mix of excitement and anxiety did a number on my emotions.

Once the two weeks were up, I went in to get my blood drawn to test my levels. It was in the fall, so I was out picking pumpkins when the nurse called with the results.

"I'm sorry," she said, "but you're not pregnant. You should be starting your cycle in a day or two."

She was kind. Her words were careful and gentle. But that didn't change the fact that this was a major blow. Cal and I were both crushed. We had hoped this was it— that this would be our month—but it wasn't. We had the option to try a few more IUI cycles or move forward with IVF, but we had to time it right. It had to be the off-season for the greenhouse.

They only had IVF sessions at certain times of the year, and they had to start the process six weeks in advance. The next one wasn't until January.

We made our choice and got on the schedule for IVF in January of 2013.

STILL TRYING

November 2012 – February 2013

THEY GIVE YOU A MANUAL TO READ ABOUT how the IVF process works. I was very overwhelmed right away. There was so much information—so many drugs that I would be taking and so many shots. IVF normally takes a few months before you will hopefully get those two pink lines on a pregnancy test.

First, they start you out on birth control for four weeks. This is so that they can get your cycle timed correctly, and to suppress your ovaries before they are stimulated. When the timing is right, that's when you start injections to stimulate your ovaries to produce as many mature eggs as you can before the egg retrieval process. The retrieval is a minor surgical process they do at the fertility clinic. It has to be timed just right, which is why they monitor everything so closely.

Many ultrasounds and blood draws are required throughout the IVF process. The doctors need to monitor your eggs while you're on medication to make sure over-stimulation is not happening. They also watch to determine when it's time for the egg retrieval process. Once the eggs are retrieved, they are placed in a special container with the fertilization sample. The eggs are then monitored, and the best viable embryos—generally one or two of them—are placed into the uterus three to five days after the retrieval. Then, you wait ten to fourteen days to see if the implantation was successful.

I went to the pharmacy to pick up everything I needed for the IVF process, and I left with two grocery bags—each packed to the brim. And that wasn't all. I had to do another test before I could proceed with IVF. Can you guess what it was?

Another dye test.

This one was to make sure my uterus was ready to have an embryo implant. I braced myself for it again. I didn't know if it would be similar to the Fallopian tube one or not, and I didn't have the same doctor doing this procedure.

I steeled myself. She started. And I felt like I was being tortured.

This test hurt *so* bad. But in my head, I kept reminding myself:

You need to do this.

Do you want to get pregnant?

It will hopefully be over soon.

She didn't ask me if I was okay this time. I don't know if I could have answered, even through clenched teeth, but then it was over. My uterus was ready. I could proceed with starting my shots to stimulate my ovaries.

This wasn't something the clinic did *for* me, either. I had to do the shots myself at home. I started with one to two shots a day and ended the process with three shots a day. I found the best way to take my shot was in my outer thigh. I felt the least amount of pain there. I would squeeze my outer thigh and push the needle in as quickly as possible.

The first time I had to give myself a shot, Shayla was at the house. I had told her what I needed to do.

"I don't know if I can do it," I said.

"I can do it for you." She's a great friend.

But she went to poke the needle in, and I yelled "NO!"

I think it was something about not being in control. As I watched her and waited for the pinch, the pain, I couldn't let her do it.

"I think I need to do it," I told her.

She was probably relieved that she didn't have to go through with it. But I am so grateful to her for being willing to try.

After about a half hour of trying to give myself that first shot, I finally did it. It wasn't as bad as I had thought it would be, but it still wasn't the greatest feeling. After about five days of shots, both of my outer thighs were lined with tiny bruises.

For eight to twelve days after starting the shots for IVF, I had to go in for an ultrasound and blood work every other day. They needed to test my estrogen levels and make sure my ovaries weren't overstimulated. I also had to start taking a shot to prevent premature ovulation.

I ended up running out of this drug too soon. It wasn't time for my egg retrieval yet, and I started to panic because the local pharmacy—where I got all of my medication—was out. It would take a day or two to get more.

Aunt June and I started calling all the pharmacies in the area to see if they had the medication in stock. After about fifteen calls, we finally found one that had it. It was two hours away. I hopped in the car and drove straight there. I couldn't let everything we had already done be for nothing and bring the IVF cycle to a halt.

I had my last ultrasound and my eggs were finally ready for retrieval. We got the call and had to be there the next morning. It was an eight-hour drive to the clinic, so we got on the road shortly after we got the call.

When we got to the egg retrieval center, we had to sit in the waiting room and wait to be called back. Another couple was leaving at the same time. She must have just had hers—her husband was helping her walk and she was hunched over and looked like she was in a lot of pain.

Cal and I looked at each other, eyes wide. My heart started to pound. What was about to happen? Would this be worse than the HSG?

They called our names; no turning back now. Even so, amidst the worry, I was also excited. We were one step closer to hopefully becoming pregnant. We had to do this.

While they were getting me set up with my IV, Cal had to go down and give his sample so that when they retrieved my eggs, they would be ready to make embryos. Cal couldn't be with me during the egg retrieval, but the nurse I had was very nice.

"As soon as the doctor is ready to start the retrieval process, I'll give you some pain medicine," she told me.

They couldn't give it to me too early because it could reduce the egg quality. Once everything was ready and it was time to start, the nurse injected the medication into my IV. Instantly, I felt the best buzz I had ever experienced.

"If you start to feel any pain let me know and I'll give you another dose," the nurse said.

Then the doctor got started. I could feel the jabbing, like he was poking my eggs out of me, so I said "Okay, I think I need some more!"

I was so tense. It didn't take too long, probably around fifteen minutes, but it was a *long* fifteen minutes.

On my way back to the recovery room where Cal was waiting for me, I was definitely still feeling good from the pain meds. Feeling loopy and giggly, I waved to everyone that I passed as they wheeled me back to my room.

They retrieved fourteen eggs that day. Nine of them were fertilized and seven of those were viable embryos. Five days later, we did a fresh embryo transfer. To improve our chances, we decided to transfer two embryos, in case one didn't take. The embryo transfer was quick and painless; after that we were on our way back home, hoping and praying for the whole eight-hour trip that our embryos would take, and we would be pregnant.

I was very miserable the next two weeks. After retrieval, your ovaries fill with fluid, which causes bloating. I was so bloated and uncomfortable from the procedure that I ate all the fiber I could get my hands on. I didn't start feeling better until ten days later, and by then I was already watching for signs to know if I was pregnant or not. That was its own kind of torture, just like the two-week wait after the IUI process. I hadn't forgotten the crushing disappointment from back then, either.

Thirteen days after our embryo transfer, I started spotting. As with everything else, this sent my emotions into a tailspin. Could this be implantation bleeding? Or was I starting my cycle? I was trapped between anxious hope and suffocating fear.

The next day I started my cycle. I think I went into denial. I went to the gym, got on the treadmill, and ran. I needed to escape my thoughts, my feelings—all of it. But that night, when Cal got home, all of those things were still there. We still weren't pregnant. The transfer had failed.

I had to tell Cal, "I'm not pregnant."

I started to cry. The roller coaster of emotions that we went through—walking that fine line between hope and fear—was just too much. I felt like I couldn't do it any-more. This was not the person I wanted to be.

"You need to be with someone else, someone who can give you a family," I sobbed. I couldn't stand the idea that I was getting in the way of that for him.

Cal didn't say anything. He just hugged me. He knew I was speaking from pain and from grief in that moment, and I think he knew not to take me at my word even though he didn't know what to do to make any of it better. No one did.

Later, a nurse called from the clinic to say she was very sorry. Again.

She also called to tell us that our remaining embryos didn't make it for freezing. We scheduled a meeting with our doctor to go over the IVF results; that meeting wasn't for two weeks, so we had time to talk about what we wanted to do.

We decided we wanted to try IVF one more time.

●

Only a week after that fresh disappointment, I was invited to brunch with a small group of people. I went, but I regretted my decision not long after showing up.

Every one of them was either pregnant, had a baby, or both. I was the only one there empty handed, still crushed from IVF not working. They were all talking about their pregnancies, their kids, and their families.

I had been so excited to start a family with Cal after we got married, and now I felt like I was going to cry. The positive person I once was had become someone else—someone who couldn't fit in with this crowd. Some of them knew we had just gone through IVF and some of them didn't. There wasn't much I could do about it at the time, so I kept my visit as short as I could and left before I could crumble any further in front of them.

When I got home, Cal asked how it went. I was honest: "Not great. They were all talking about their pregnancies and babies. It wasn't easy being there."

He wasn't very happy about it either.

When the doctor called to go over our results with us, Cal was out working. I was alone. The doctor told me that our embryos had dissolved on day seven; that was probably what happened after they were transferred, too.

I remember him telling me, "There is likely something else wrong with your eggs. I recommend using an egg donor if you would like to try IVF again."

When I got off the phone, I started to sob. I had stayed hopeful up until that call. Despite the negativity and the hurt through all of those tests, procedures, and crushing disappointments, I had kept holding on to the hope that it could still happen. We could still get pregnant.

This was the first time that I felt hopeless.

I called Cal and tried to tell him through my tears. We talked about other options, like trying an egg donor. When I considered it, though, it felt like Cal would be having a baby with someone else and I would be the surrogate. Yes, I would get to experience pregnancy, but that wasn't the way I wanted it to happen. If I was going to carry a baby, then I wanted the baby to be a part of both of us. Cal agreed with me.

The next option that made the most sense was adoption. When we talked, it felt like we were both on the same page about it, so a week later I started to research agencies to find out our options. I was still crushed and disappointed. But I guess, even then, I hadn't stopped hoping. I was still looking to the horizon, hoping against all hope. I was on the lookout for a rainbow, and I wasn't going to give up until I had exhausted every option.

ADOPTION

February – December 2013

I COULDN'T SIT AROUND AND WAIT OR SLEEP on it. Not doing anything was worse than trying to push through regular, everyday life while holding this pain inside of me all the time. Why did I have to be the one to struggle so hard just to have a family? I felt hopeless and broken after that round of IVF failed. It felt brutally unfair. Why couldn't my body just do what it was supposed to be able to do?

I could have taken some time to grieve and process what we were going through, but back then I didn't want to take a break. There was something desperate but also comforting about continuing to reach for that goal that we had—the goal of starting a family together. I couldn't bring myself to stop or slow down.

I researched interstate adoption first. If all fifty states were open to us, we could hopefully find a match quickly. But not only was this option expensive—$20,000 to $30,000—it was also time consuming. If we got a match through an agency in another state, we would have to stay in that state with the baby until the birth family could go to a court hearing where they would terminate their parental rights. Until that happened, the adoption wouldn't be official. It could take anywhere from three days to two weeks. We knew that if we happened to get a match during greenhouse season or pumpkin patch season, we wouldn't be able to be away for that long. And the cost—after spending so much on IVF recently—that was a hard pill to swallow.

I looked into local adoption agencies next, hoping to adopt in our state, and there were only two options available. The limitation didn't make me feel very hopeful, but I had a look. Between the two agencies, one had a Catholic background and the other was Lutheran. I was raised in the Lutheran tradition, so that was enough to give me a nudge in their direction.

I called The Village Family Service Center and ended up on the phone with someone who went over some of the adoption process with me. She talked through the timeline for all the things we'd have to accomplish just to get set up with the agency. Then she told me she would send more information for me to look over.

I got off the phone and began to cry. The process was so overwhelming. The home study alone would take at least three months. Home studies are required for all adoptions, and they generally consist of interviews with your social worker. Cal and I would have interviews together with the social worker as well as individually. The agency wants to understand the nature of your relationship with your partner and what your home life is like.

During the home study, a social worker would come to our home for a few visits to see where we lived. They would check our finances to make sure we would be able to provide for a child. They would do background checks for any criminal history, and we would have to have medical checkups done. Blood work and x-rays were required for both of us.

The Village also sent out paperwork to five references, asking their opinion about Cal and me having a family and what we're both like. We would both have to attend a weekend full of adoption classes. Then, after we had checked off everything on our home-study list, our social worker would write up a report of all of it. That report would be used by the adoption agency and in court hearings for finalizing the adoption.

One of the hardest things in all of this is that, once the whole process is over, it doesn't even guarantee anything. It turns into a waiting game: you have to wait until someone picks your family.

We had already been waiting so long, hoping for something to happen. Now we had to continue to wait through another very long process. There was no point in making it take any longer than it already would, so we started to move forward with the adoption process and got back to life at the greenhouse in the meantime. There was no pretending everything was normal, but we could at least fall into some rhythms that *felt* normal while we waited.

I was helping full time at the green-house by then. I helped Aunt June do the watering every day, though I'm not sure how she was still able to do it. I was completely exhausted at the end of each day, and she was still going pretty strong despite being fifty-nine years old. When I first started helping out, I thought watering would be one of the easier jobs.

Was I ever wrong.

Dragging a hose all day is so tiring. Certain plants need more water than others, and when they're first starting to grow you have to check each individual plant to make sure you're not over-watering them. When coleus plants are first growing, for example, if you even look at them, they'll rot.

The month of May at the greenhouse is a very hard month to get through as well. We're at maximum capacity, and there's so much to take care of and water. This is also when we start to get really busy with customers.

It was mainly family working at the time, so we worked every day with no days off. We all had our jobs to do and they needed to be done every day. We would try to start watering early, around 7:00 a.m., so that we could finish up in the sales area by the time it was open to customers. That way, we could stay out of their way during the day and finish up the watering in the other greenhouses. Watering took six to eight hours and after everything was watered, I would help customers and try to stock as much as I could.

By 9:00 p.m. we would still be stocking. At that point, I could hardly take another step. We'd go home, sit down for a bit, then go straight to bed only to get up and do it all over again the next day. I can still remember how my feet felt when I got out of bed in the mornings: like walking on pins and needles. My body was still too exhausted from the day before. I've said this many times: if it's my time to go during greenhouse season, I want my gravestone to say, "She didn't survive the season!"

But that grueling day-to-day cycle didn't let me sit down long enough to think. It might have been the best way for me to get through the season of waiting. It took ten months after we started the adoption process before it was time to move on to the next step of the journey: creating our adoption profile book.

Until we had our book up on The Village website, we couldn't even be considered for adoption. The book gives birth families a glimpse into our life. The families look through adoption profile books when they're deciding on an adoptive family to meet to see if they want to make an adoption plan together.

I put so much pressure on myself about this book. It felt like so much was riding on it. This was the book that could bring us our family. This was the book that would let a birth family get to know us. This book had to represent us—and our life—perfectly.

That pressure didn't help me get started. I procrastinated for a while, like any good college student trying to write a heavily weighted paper. Where was I supposed to begin? I had to find the right words— the perfect words. And pictures—which pictures should I use? It took me a week before I finally sat down at the computer and got started.

And I didn't stop for three days straight. I sat at that computer, picking out the words and images that would give us our chance. I don't know how I would have gotten it done if it wasn't during our off-season in

December. The daily grind of greenhouse season certainly wouldn't have made it any easier.

My years of experience in photography helped with picking photos, sure, but that was only a part of it. I still had to write about us, and there was nothing like that to help me find just the right words. I had to dig deep, and I second-guessed myself at every turn. The pursuit of perfection can be a relentless, overwhelming monster, and I'm not sure how many times I fought against it during those three days.

How would this phrase make us sound to another family?

What about this word here?

Could this ruin a potential chance with a family?

The only thing that pulled me through was imagining that end goal. I didn't have to remind myself what I was aiming for—I had been fighting for this ever since Cal and I got married, and I wasn't about to stop now.

So, I sat at the computer, Cal brought me food, and I finished our adoption profile book one page at a time.

A CHANCE

J ANUARY 2014, A YEAR AFTER OUR IVF CYCLE failed, our adoption profile book was uploaded to The Village website. Now came the hardest part of the whole process: waiting for The Call.

It was another waiting game.

This was a big year for us, and not just because we were set up to hopefully adopt. This was the year Cal had been working toward ever since eighth grade. His dream of owning the greenhouse was finally coming true. He was taking over!

I was so happy for him at the time, but I also knew how big the responsibility for the greenhouse was. There would be so much more pressure with ownership on top of the regular work—so much to care for and so many living things. Jerry and June said they would help us for the first few years to make sure we had everything under control, which was very generous of them, but it was still going to be a massive undertaking.

We got to work. I took over bookkeeping since Cal wanted one of us to know what was going on with that at all times. I tried to get that all figured out, while taking on management of scheduling and hiring staff at the same time. We also had to open new accounts, which was pretty much like starting a business from scratch.

Our daily work at the greenhouse wasn't going to change that much. We knew what we had to do. The biggest shift, mentally perhaps, was that now it would be on us if anything happened or went wrong. Cal would be making the decisions. He could always ask Jerry for advice, of course, but I think they even started to butt heads a few times. I'm sure the transition wasn't easy for Jerry—he had been the one making all the decisions up until that point—but he made it work and we knew he just wanted the greenhouse to thrive.

By April, we had been running things for just over three months. We were still learning how to manage everything and keep on top of the work, but we had fallen into our own kind of routine. I was busy enough to stay distracted, but not enough that I had forgotten the other goal we were working toward.

On April 4th, I was busy watering as usual. I had an interview scheduled with a local news station to test out a new pocket hose, and the greenhouse tasks were keeping me on my feet. It wasn't until around lunchtime that I realized I couldn't find my phone.

I flew into a panic. Where had I left my phone? I started looking everywhere. I knew better than to leave it lying around. I was distracted, but I knew we were waiting for a phone call. I knew I needed to keep my phone close. Besides, you never want to leave anything on the benches at the greenhouse; you may not find it again until the end of the season.

I still hadn't found it and I was getting frantic. I finally found Cal and asked him to call it for me—and I heard it! I ran up and down the aisles and finally found it. I had left it in between the tall elephant ears. I looked at the screen.

Missed call from . . . our social worker!

My heart sank into my belly, and I started to shake. Was this it? Were we getting The Call? What if I'd missed our chance? I was excited and terrified. I didn't know what to think. The watering would have to wait. I called her back. I couldn't believe I'd missed this call.

She answered right away. "Hi, Ashley! Is Cal with you?"

"I'll go get him." I ran over to where he was taking his lunch break and put the phone on speaker.

"So, we have a birth mother who is very serious about making an adoption plan," she said. "She wants to meet you both."

Oh my goodness. Four months—after four months we got the call that we'd been wishing and hoping for. I could hardly believe it was happening. I had heard of families having to wait so much longer and a part of me didn't want to let myself feel excited because nothing had happened yet— nothing was for sure. But there was also nothing that could stop the spark of hope from lighting up in my chest again. I couldn't help it. This could actually be it—our chance.

Our social worker told us a little bit about the birth family and their circumstances. "I know this is not a great time for you guys," she added. She knew we were right in the middle of greenhouse season. "You think about it and get back to me."

We didn't have to think about it for very long. It wasn't going to be easy to keep on top of things and get everything at the greenhouse organized while we started this next step of the process. But how could we say no? What if we never got picked again?

This baby was going to be with us forever—our family. We just needed to make it through a few busy months.

The next Monday we drove four hours to the local adoption agency to meet the birth family. We had to have separate meetings with the birth mother and birth father; they were no longer together. The birth father didn't want the adoption to happen. He was willing to meet with us, but this wouldn't have been his choice.

When it was time to meet the birth mother, Kara, she was waiting for us in the room with her mom. There was also a social worker there while we visited, to help the meeting along.

I was so nervous. I wanted to show the real me, but I didn't want to say the wrong things. Between advice to "just be yourself" and the fear that any slip up might lead the family to think we weren't a good fit, I was a ball of nerves.

In the end, they were very easy to talk to. The meeting went smoothly, and Kara and her mother said they loved our profile book. They said we did a great job. I felt so validated; like all of the pressure and the time that I took to get each page just right had paid off. During the meeting, Kara told us why she wanted to make an adoption plan and she let us know that the baby would be a boy.

"Ashley, I want you to be in the birthing room with me. He'll go straight to you," she said.

I felt so overwhelmed at that moment, thinking about holding him for the first time, with her right there in the hospital room. The plan was that we would have our own room at the hospital and care for him the whole hospital stay. Kara didn't want to see the baby until everything was finalized and she went to court. She signed her Termination of Parental Rights papers through the adoption agency so that the court hearing could proceed more quickly, and everything just felt right. Despite the nerves, anxiety, and worry piled on by the previous failures and struggles we had gone through, I felt that this adoption was meant to be.

We all took our first picture together and then we met with Aden—the father—and his parents.

Aden was hard to read. I'm not sure if he was nervous or just didn't want the adoption to happen, but we talked more with his parents than we did with him. The social worker tried to get him to talk but he only said a few words.

He was honest. He told us that he didn't agree with the adoption, but he knew it was for the best and would try to move forward. They were both so young—still in high school. I couldn't even begin to imagine what this must have felt like for them.

By the end of the meeting, he started to warm up a bit. We left the agency feeling good about it all. That spark of hope in my chest was growing and everything we had been hoping for all these months seemed like it might actually come true. Soon, we might finally start our family.

We were going to grab a bite to eat before we headed back on our drive home, but as we were driving, I noticed a baby store. It was as if there was a halo around it, like it was glowing.

"Oh my goodness, Cal! We have to stop there!"

I don't think I could have done anything to stifle the excitement growing inside of me, even if it was too soon, and even if I should have played it safe and waited just a bit longer.

I couldn't help it.

Cal pulled into the lot and stopped. I was so excited I could hardly get my seatbelt off fast enough. I walked in and got all the butterflies. There were so many cute things. I ended up buying the most adorable, tiny, blue shoes, a diaper bag, and two of the softest onesies I had ever touched. I had waited four years to buy baby clothes and I was taking the experience *all in*. I didn't want to miss a single thing.

The social worker called us on our drive home to tell us that the birth families were both still on board. Kara felt great after the meeting. Aden was still not quite there yet, but they felt he would be with time.

Kara was due April 28th. We had about three weeks to wait. Kara and I texted back and forth to get to know one another better. She sent ultrasound pictures of her last appointment. It was so hard to wait even just those three short weeks. Hope was blossoming and growing into something real and tangible—something I felt we could almost touch. We had to wait just a little bit longer, but this adoption was moving forward.

We were so excited to meet him!

OUR FIRST BABY

April – May 2014

I GOT A TEXT FROM KARA ON TUESDAY, APRIL 29th. She told me that they were going to induce labor the next morning.

We got everything in line at the greenhouse and packed the car so we'd be ready to leave early in the morning. We got a hotel room where we could wait until they were ready for us to come to the hospital, which didn't end up being until about eight o'clock that night. Kara had changed her mind about me being in the delivery room. I was fine with that—I wanted her to be comfortable—so they put Cal and me in a room right next door where we waited some more.

At 9:34 pm, he was born. The nurses brought him right over to us. He was all curled up in a ball. I could hardly see him. They put him on the scale right away—eight pounds, ten ounces—and Cal cut his umbilical cord. He was perfect. We named him Kip Cooper and I started crying just from looking at him. I couldn't believe how much I loved him already after just meeting him. We were finally parents!

After he was cleaned up a little, we even fed him his first bottle. Both Cal and I just stared at him, memorizing every feature of his tiny face. We took pictures to send to some of our family and friends. It was one of the most incredible moments of my life. I didn't understand how I could love someone so much after such a short amount of time, but I wasn't going to question it. This was it: our first child. Our Kip Cooper.

As much joy as I was feeling, I was also wondering how Kara was doing. I kept asking the nurses about her. Adoption isn't easy. It's difficult for me to even imagine what she must have been feeling. My heart was pulling me constantly in two different directions: I was so, so happy to meet Kip and to hold him, but my heart was also aching. I knew Kara, Aden, and their families were grieving. They were going through a loss.

We were moved to a new room right next to Kara's room where we would be for the rest of our hospital stay. We hardly got any sleep that night. It was so hard for me to let myself fall asleep. I had to make sure Kip was okay at all times. We fed him every two hours. The nurses placed the bassinet as close to my bed as they could, and they were in and out of our room all night.

The next morning, I texted Kara to see how she was. I asked if I could come visit her for a bit. I had bought her a gift that I wanted to give to her. My thinking was that if I had been the one to just give birth, I would want to wear the most comfortable sweat outfit ever. I learned she liked the Victoria's Secret PINK line the first time we met, so I had found her a PINK one. I also framed the picture we had taken together for her to have.

I went to see her and asked her how she was feeling.

"Pretty good," she said. She asked how Kip was doing. I told her he was doing great and eating well.

"How are you feeling about everything?" I asked. "Does everything still feel right to you?" I hadn't let myself think about the dread I would feel if she answered with anything other than "yes." It was almost inconceivable at this point, after having met Kip—after having held him and fallen in love with him already. She looked comfortable while we were talking and seemed to be processing everything well.

"I'm so very happy with my decision," Kara said. She seemed so calm and positive about everything. At the time, I took that as a good sign. I may have even felt a little bit of relief. "Thank you for giving him a better life for me."

Beth, the social worker who was working with us, came up to check on everyone at the hospital and to make sure everything was going smoothly. She made sure to ask Kara quite a few times if she wanted to see Kip and that she should let us know if she did.

Aden came to the hospital with his parents. They hung out in our room for the majority of the day and we got to know each other better. I could tell Aden was getting ready for this adoption to happen. He even signed the Termination of Parental Rights papers while Beth was there. Then they left for a while and said they would be back later.

While they were gone, Kara's mom wanted to come over and meet Kip. She wanted to hold him for a while. She was still there holding him when, about fifteen minutes later, there was a knock at our door. It was Kara.

She wanted to come in, just to see him. She also brought us a diaper cake for him.

"I don't want to hold him," she assured me. "I just want to hang out for a while and see him."

We were fine with whatever she wanted. We didn't want her to regret her time at the hospital, so she spent some time with Kip.

It was later, around supper time, when Kara sent another text.

"My grandma is coming up and wants to meet Kip. Is it okay if I bring him to my room for a few hours?"

Kip had been at our side all night and all day now. We hadn't been away from him yet. I could feel the separation anxiety settling in. Was she having second thoughts? She didn't say anything about it. But she had said before that she didn't want to see him, so the fact that she changed her mind about that made me nervous.

But of course, we agreed. The experience she was going through had to be hard enough and I knew I would want to do everything in my power to ensure I didn't regret my time at the hospital if I was the one in her position.

Cal and I decided to go for supper to take our minds off things and just get away for a little bit. When we got back, Kip was still with Kara. We settled into the hospital room again to wait.

We waited and waited and waited. It felt like such a long time. My stomach started to tie itself into knots. I felt sick. We had been so careful to check in with Kara all this time to make sure we were all still on the same page and she was comfortable with her decision. But what if that changed? I'd hardly let myself think about it. I didn't think I could bear how painful that would be after everything.

Finally, Kara sent a text. "I'm sorry I'm keeping him longer than I thought! I just need to have him so I can say goodbye tomorrow."

I breathed a sigh of relief. Not knowing was worse than anything else, so that small reassurance affected me deeply. I told her to take all the time she needed, and we brought him over to our room about a half hour later.

After spending another night with Kip, Cal and I woke up excited. Today was the day we would bring our son home! I went downstairs for an iced coffee and sent Kara a text asking her if she wanted one.

There was no reply.

When I got back up to the room, Cal was sitting next to the bassinet. Kip was lying there, bundled up and sleeping peacefully. But I could tell something wasn't right.

"Beth was here," he said. "Kara is having second thoughts."

My stomach dropped and twisted back into those painful knots. I couldn't take another sip of coffee. I felt so sick.

"Her mom is on a walk with her right now, talking to her," Cal said.

I looked over at Kip and started to cry.

Cal came over and wrapped me in a hug. "We don't know for sure yet," he said softly. But his voice was rough. I knew he was just as scared as I was.

Another half hour later, Beth knocked on our door. She came in and said the words that we were both dreading. Every sentence was like a punch in the gut:

"I am so very sorry.

I don't have good news.

She changed her mind."

Cal and I instantly began to cry. I felt like my heart was being ripped out. How could this be happening? After everything else we had already gone through, how could this happen to us now?

"You've spent a lot of time with him. You've bonded with him," Beth said. I think she knew we needed the reminder. We weren't in any frame of mind to think straight. "Take all the time you need to say goodbye."

Aden and his parents were waiting outside. They wanted to know if it would be alright to come in and say goodbye to us as well. We had spent all day yesterday getting to know them. When they came in, everyone was just crying. Aden and his parents each gave us a hug. They told us how sorry they were. Aden was finally ready to see this adoption happen—but Kara changed her mind.

Eventually, it was time. There was nothing we could do. We had taken all the steps. I had put my care and energy behind every page of that adoption profile book. I had tried to word everything perfectly—tried to create the perfect picture of the home

Cal and I would provide for any child we matched with. And in the end, it still wasn't enough.

I was crying as I said goodbye to Kip. I kissed him on his forehead. That was all there was left to do.

Before we left, Beth tried to give me back the gift I had bought for Kara. Kara said she didn't feel right taking it, but I didn't want it back. I had picked it out especially for her—another place where I had spent my energy and tried so hard to make everything perfect. I didn't need any extra reminders of this nightmare. I think I told Beth to throw it away. Then Cal and I grabbed our suitcase and the empty car seat and made our way to the elevator.

I tried to stay somewhat composed as we were riding down in the elevator, but I couldn't. There were other people in there with us, but I just kept sobbing. I stared and stared at the empty car seat, knowing that Kip should be in there. I felt gutted and empty and I couldn't see straight through my tears.

It was a quiet drive for the two of us. On the way home, we stopped to fill up and go to the restroom, and I will never forget the way

I felt walking into that gas station. I felt as if I was walking in slow motion. My legs were so heavy. It was like all the life had been sucked out of me.

We had a swing, a bassinet, and a changing table set up at our house. We were fully ready for the day when we were supposed to come home with Kip. Before we got back, I asked some of our friends and family to take it down. I didn't want to have to see it when we got home.

We came home to an empty house. I had an equally empty feeling inside. It was like I had nothing left to give. Some part of me had been ripped away and I didn't know if I'd ever get it back again.

"I'm going to go check on the greenhouse," Cal said. We'd barely made it through the door. "Are you going to be okay for a bit if I leave?"

"Yes," I said. There was nothing he or I could do to make this nightmare any better.

I can't really remember what I did after that. When Cal came back in from the greenhouse, we watched some TV. Then I said, "I'm going to bed."

"Okay," he said. "I'm going to stay up for a bit."

The emptiness I was feeling still took up so much space in the house. I could feel it as I climbed the stairs. I still felt heavy— weighed down by something almost physical—as I got ready for bed.

I had just laid my head down on the pillow when I heard Cal crying. I got up right away. I went back downstairs and found him looking at pictures of Kip. I walked right to him and hugged him, closing the distance that had grown between us in the silence of our grief.

"I miss him," Cal sobbed. He could hardly talk through the tears.

I've only seen Cal cry a few times since we've been together. The last time was on Christmas day in 2008; we had just got down to my mom's place to celebrate with them. We had been with Cal's family the night before. A half hour after we got to my mom's, Breanna called. Cal had only been on the phone for a few seconds when he waved for me to follow him downstairs to where no one was around. He sat in a chair and when the phone call ended, he looked up at me. He could hardly hold my gaze.

"My dad is gone," he said. "He committed suicide."

He put his face in his hands and cried.

I hurried over to him to hold him, just as I was doing now. He had lost his father then. This time, we had lost a child. I wanted to take away his pain that time too, but there was nothing I could do. I just tried to be there for him. My heart was hurting so bad this time as well, and it hurt all the more because he was hurting with me.

When Cal's dad died, we said goodbye to my family and got back on the road so he could be with his brother and sister. This time, there was nowhere for us to go. There was no one we wanted to surround ourselves with to try to soften the edge of the pain. It was just us—Cal and me—alone in our too-empty house.

ONE STEP AT A TIME

May – October 2014

THE DAY AFTER WE GOT BACK FROM THE hospital, we had to go back to work at the greenhouse.

I didn't want to go. I had no drive to do anything. I was walking up the sidewalk to get my watering started for the day and I looked over to where Jerry was playing soccer with his two grandsons. I started to cry. I was supposed to have a son right now. I was supposed to watch him grow up and eventually play soccer like they were.

It was a constant battle to hold myself together all day. When June came up to me a little while later and asked how I was doing, I tried to hold back the tears, but they came streaming down.

Everything about Kip was engraved into my brain. The way he smelled, the way he cried, the hiccupping and burping sounds he made.

June wiped away some of my tears. I tried to keep going for the day, but I couldn't. I just didn't have any energy. All I wanted to do was cry and I couldn't shake the feeling that everyone was moving forward, carrying on with their lives, and we were heartbroken again.

I told Cal I needed to go home for the rest of the day. I apologized, but if he wasn't going to be understanding, who was? We both knew the greenhouse work didn't stop for anything. We both also knew just how much pain the other person was feeling. And maybe that was how each of us coped; Cal gave himself to his work for distraction, and I needed to wrap myself up in quiet and rest.

I may not have seen it that way at the time. It felt more like giving up, like I couldn't handle it in the moment and I was letting Cal down. But grief doesn't answer to the day-to-day grind. Cal and I had to learn how grief affected us as individuals, even as we fought to hold each other together through it all. Grief built up inside of Cal like pent-up energy that he had to let out through his work; but grief sucked me dry. It was all I could do to just keep moving through my day. I needed to pause and breathe.

So, I went home. Shortly after, Breanna sent me a text to ask how I was.

"Not good," I answered. "But a little better now that I'm home."

There was nothing else I could bring myself to say. I don't know if slowing down and trying to rest was any better for me. It didn't matter what I did—I couldn't stop thinking about him.

Kip. Our Kip—our baby boy.

I had to try to see him. I couldn't think of any other way to fill the gaping emptiness that I felt inside of me as the heavy silence of the house settled around me. I didn't think about how seeing him might make everything worse. I just knew that I missed him.

I checked Kara's Facebook page to look for a picture of him. I shouldn't have, but I couldn't stop myself. She had a bunch of pictures of him, with captions about how happy she was. She had named him. And it wasn't the same name that we had given him. It wasn't Kip.

How could it seem like she didn't care about what she had just done to us? She never had to face us again. She would never have to give us any kind of explanation. She walked away from this with a family. Did she even care that she had left us empty-handed?

Did she even know?

The next day, I called Beth. I was crying again. Maybe I had been crying all along. The stages of grief all blurred together, but when I spoke with her, I was in the bargaining stage.

"Please tell her to bring him back to us," I said through more tears. "We miss him so much! Tell her to change her mind, again. Please!"

"I'm so sorry for the pain you're going through right now," Beth said. She tried to talk me down. "I'm so sorry, Ashley. I wish I could change things for you both."

But, of course, there was nothing she could do. There was nothing anyone could do to bring Kip back to us.

Over the next few days and weeks, I replayed everything in my head over and over. Why hadn't she changed her mind before we met him? Why had she let it go that far? She had reassured us so many times that this adoption was going to happen. She had put Kip in our arms; she had let us feed him, hold him, and fall in love with him. How could she do that and then take it all away?

I didn't know that it was possible to feel so alone, while also being cared for by the people around me—because we weren't alone. I was very grateful to have our family and friends to help us get through the grief. I talked to my mom and my friend Jess almost every day. It didn't change anything or take the pain away but talking with people definitely helped.

My parents were there for me in a way that no one else could be. When I was in second grade, my parents had gotten divorced. They hardly ever talked to each other after that, but after we lost Kip, my dad called my mom. He was so concerned about me.

"We need to do something," he told Mom.

"I know," Mom said. "It's so hard to see Ashley hurting this way. But there's not much we can do. We just need to be there for them and try to get them through this."

They couldn't do anything anymore than the social worker could change what had happened. They couldn't take the pain away. But they were there for us when we needed them most, and I don't know how I would have made it through without them.

I didn't know if I wanted to keep our adoption book on The Village website at the time. How could we possibly go through this again? The thought of going through the whole process only to come out on the other side with nothing—it would break me all over.

Cal was the one who convinced me. He said, "After knowing what it feels like to be a family for two days, I know I definitely want to try again."

And he was right. We both knew we wanted this family—our family. So, we kept our book in. We didn't talk about how many times we would be willing to go through this if it happened again. I don't know if we had any of those answers. We just knew we weren't ready to give up yet.

The wait began again. There was probably some fear mixed in with the anticipation this time as we prepared ourselves to wait for The Call. We had waited four months last time, and I had heard stories of families who waited years for a match. I don't think either one of us was expecting anything right away. We thought we'd have some time to settle into our decision.

As time passed, we received cards and letters from supportive family and friends, and the notes and encouragements began to help me to move forward.

About a month after everything happened, I got a letter in the mail from Beth. She opened the letter by saying that she had gone to the local Victoria's Secret and had spoken with the manager there to explain what had happened with the gift I'd gotten for Kara. The manager was able to put the equivalent dollar value on a gift card for me.

Beth also wrote, "I know the last month has been difficult for you and Cal. I am hoping with the passage of time that you're feeling better and your hearts are starting to heal."

I don't know if the words would have struck me the same way closer to losing Kip, but after a month, I was able to hear them and let them sink in. It was encouraging to know how supportive our social worker was when we were going through this heartbreak.

I also received a letter from a lady that went to the church in my hometown. Her words helped me get up every morning and keep going.

Good morning Ashley and Cal,

This morning may not seem like a good morning since you are in pain from your great disappointment! It pains me too!

I want you to remember that the Lord does not close one door without opening another.

Have faith, courage, think positive, and your most wonderful morning will come.

Your friend,
Gertie

As the months passed by, I started to imagine the wonderful morning to come again—my rainbow on the horizon. I grew desperate for something to happen. We were healing and we wanted to get picked again. I needed to feel happy, not sad and in pain anymore. I didn't want to keep dwelling on what happened with Kip.

We headed into pumpkin patch season, and it was a hard season for me. Everyone came out as a family and I'd watch all the kids run around and think: that could have been us. That *should* have been us.

I tried to keep myself occupied with projects so that I didn't have time to think. Everyone looked so happy, while I was still living in a fog. The notes and encouragements helped—they always help—but they didn't take the pain away. I had to keep putting one foot in front of the other and keep going. I had to keep hoping for my rainbow.

MOX PARKER

October ¬ December 2014

I WAS BUSY HELPING CUSTOMERS, WEIGHING and stocking pumpkins; I was so busy I could hardly think. I had left my phone in the back and went to grab it.

Missed call from . . .

My heart sank into my belly just like it had six months ago. I'd missed a call from our social worker—again!

I called Cal right away and we called the social worker back together, hoping we could get through the phone call between customers.

The social worker picked up and said, "Ashley and Cal, I'm so happy to be the one making this phone call to you! I have a birth mother who wants to make an adoption plan. She's picked you guys!"

She told us about Faye, the birth mother. She also told us that the birth father had terminated his parental rights and wouldn't be a part of the adoption. This already felt different than the last time. Would it be less complicated since the birth father would not be part of the process? In that moment, neither Cal nor I could prevent our minds from replaying everything that had happened with Kip—but that didn't stop us either.

"Would you like to know the gender?" the social worker asked.

"Yes," we said.

"It's a boy!"

Cal and I both looked at each other and smiled. Before we got picked the first time, we would've been happy with a boy or a girl, but after losing Kip, I wanted it to be another boy. It felt right.

"Faye is hoping to get together next week sometime and, if you both are comfortable, she would like to meet with you without a social worker present. She's going to her hometown for the weekend and she could meet you on her way so it's not such a long drive for you."

Faye lived in the same town as Kara. The social worker gave me Faye's number so

I could reach out if I wanted. She told us Beth would call later to go over more details. It was a relief to know that Beth would be working with us again. She had been with us while we were going through Kip's adoption and she'd been incredibly caring and encouraging. I think I was glad to have someone familiar with us again.

About an hour after I got off the phone, I sent Faye a text. I think my mind was still fighting between excitement and fear—I knew how badly we wanted this to happen. I just needed to do something to make it all feel real for myself.

"Hi Faye, it's Ashley," I wrote. "I just wanted to let you know we are very excited to meet you next week!" When she wrote back, she said she was looking forward to meeting us too!

Later that night, Beth called. We were talking through some of the details and she said, "I need to tell you something pretty crazy. So, remember when I told you I got you that Victoria's Secret gift card with some help from the store manager? *Faye* is that manager! She has no idea, but she picked you guys!"

I could hardly believe it. If Faye had known and had ended up picking us because of that connection, maybe that would have been less shocking; but Faye had no idea we were the couple that had happened to!

I couldn't stop my mind from spinning. Was this why we had to go through the pain from the first adoption? To bring us to Faye? After all the hurt and pain we'd been going through the past six months, I finally felt like I had some reasons for *why*. I finally felt like I had answers. Now, I was hoping and praying that this was the door God was opening for us.

Ten days later we met Faye at a Starbucks. She had sent us a picture of herself, so we knew who to look for. I was so nervous again. My stomach was in knots and I couldn't get the jitters out of my system. The first meetings are always such an intense roller coaster of emotions. The hope, the fear, the sheer possibility that this might be what we had been waiting for, for so many years—there was no taming those feelings. We had to settle into them and let things play out. And to do that, we had to keep hoping.

We walked in and spotted her right away. Faye had long, blonde, wavy hair and the most beautiful smile and complexion. She was already sitting at a table. We sat down and started to make conversation. It's hard to remember what we all talked about, but some moments stood out.

She told us why she wanted to make an adoption plan. "I love him very much. I know I can raise him, but I want more for him. I want him to have a mom and a dad all the time. When I was looking at all the profile books and I came to yours, I knew instantly that I wanted to meet you. I didn't even have to open the book up."

It sounded like a dream come true. Was this even real? Could this be happening? I told her about us trying to get pregnant for some time, and Faye said the most amazing thing someone could have said to us: "I want to be the vessel to bring you your family."

She was the one to heal our hearts.

She showed us a picture of her last ultrasound and that's when we got to see him for the first time. He had the cutest button nose. She told us we could keep the picture. I stared at it the whole drive home. I didn't know it was possible to feel this happy.

After we left Starbucks, Cal and I both felt really great about the meeting with Faye.

Beth called us later and said Faye felt the same. My heart was filled with hope again.

As excited as we wanted to let ourselves get, we knew we needed to protect ourselves this time. We wouldn't tell anyone anything until we were on the way home from the hospital. Last time too many people knew. It made the pain that much harder to bear. People were asking how our son was doing and we had to keep telling them that it didn't work out. We had to keep reliving the heartbreak over and over, every time someone asked. We knew we didn't want to go through that again.

But keeping a secret from people you love and trust isn't easy. Even in a case like this, there can be some merit in having other people who know and love you walk alongside you for the journey.

I met my friend Jess to go for a walk one day. We were chatting and after about ten minutes she said, "I have to tell you something."

Instantly, my reaction was, "Are you pregnant?!"

She and her husband had been married for seven years. They'd wanted to wait to start a family and they had traveled for work ever since they got married. But I knew it was only a matter of time.

"No," she said, "but I do want to let you know that we are going to start trying. I wanted to give you a heads up."

It was amazing of her to be thinking of my feelings. She knew how hard it had been for me not to get pregnant. So many people don't think about what it's like for those struggling with infertility to watch their friends and family have their own kids and grow their families right alongside them. Jess showed me such an incredible amount of understanding and respect in that moment.

So, naturally, I felt really bad about not telling her what was happening in our lives. I had wanted to tell her from the very start, but I wanted to protect myself. It was like I was holding a secret wish inside of me. I had looked up to the sky at that shooting star, blown out the candles on that birthday cake, and made my wish. And I felt like if I told anyone, my wish wouldn't come true.

But with Jess, after about ten minutes, I couldn't take it any longer. I spewed it all out. She was there for me so much after the first adoption and I wanted her with me through this one too.

It felt so good to tell her, and she took it well. She was shocked at first—it was hard to believe that we both had such big news for each other on the same walk—but after the initial excitement wore off, she had to remember what had happened last time, just like I did. Even though it was nerve wracking and frightening, it still felt so good to have Jess on my side. I knew she would be praying and supporting us through all of the next steps.

It was a seven-week wait until Faye's due date. Cal and I had a trip planned for three weeks before the due date. We went back and forth on whether we should go. What if she went into labor while we were gone, and we couldn't get back?

We waited to hear about her last doctor's appointment to know if she could possibly go into labor early. Everything looked right on time, so we ended up going on the trip, but I had to fight to let myself enjoy the experience. Most of the time, I was thinking about Faye and the baby. And when we got back home, I pretty much barricaded myself in the house, just waiting for the call. I was too worried to do anything in case it would be time and we would need to go.

I finally started to drive myself crazy, so I booked a facial to get out and try to relax. She hadn't called me yet, so I figured she wouldn't call in the hour I was gone. That day, Cal ended up going hunting not too far from town.

I knew the girl that was doing my facial. She had heard about our first adoption not working out, and while we were making small talk, she asked how the adoption process was going. I played it safe. I told her we were just waiting to get picked again.

About halfway through my facial my phone rang.

"Do you need to get that?"

I tried but ended up missing the call anyway, and when I looked, I saw:

Missed call from Faye.

I scrambled to call her back right away. My heart dropped into my stomach as it always did and then she picked up.

"I've been in labor since last night and I think it's time for you guys to come!" she said. She'd been having some painful contractions and was taking a lot of baths. I told her I wished I could take the pain away.

The girl doing my facial had heard most of my conversation with Faye. I got off the phone and turned to her, ready to bolt.

"Remember twenty minutes ago when you asked about the adoption process?" I said. "Well, I kind of fibbed to you. We did get picked again and she is in labor!"

She was very excited for us. She washed the stuff off my face and I asked her to keep the news to herself.

"Of course!" she said. She waved at me as I was running out the door to my car.

I called Cal on the way home and told him to meet me back at the house. I could hardly keep calm as I drove. We packed our last-minute things in a whirlwind and got back in the car for the four-hour drive to the hospital.

It was excruciating—having to sit still that whole drive, all the while worrying that we were going to be late. I tried to distract myself while Cal drove, but I couldn't focus on anything besides my racing thoughts. I don't think either of us knew what to say, but eventually Cal voiced the thought that had been haunting us both:

"This has to work, right? This can't happen to us twice . . ."

But there was no way to know, and there was nothing left for us to do but drive and keep holding on to hope.

When we got there, Faye said she was not progressing, so they were going to do a C-section. We'd made it in time!

We got set up in the waiting room and Faye's friend came in to talk to us for a bit. He asked if we were excited. We said yes, but that we were trying not to get *too* excited. He had heard what happened with our first adoption.

"That's very understandable," he told us.

After about fifteen minutes, a nurse came in. "Faye is wondering if you'd like to come back and talk for a bit."

"Yes! Of course," we said. So, we went back, and I asked her how she was doing.

"Pretty good! I'm excited to meet him. How are you guys feeling?"

"We're very excited to meet him too!"

The combination of emotions that Cal and I were both feeling in that moment was almost indescribable. The nerves and anxiety mixed with rushes of excitement made us feel like we were kids lining up for a theme park ride. Were we really doing this? Were we going through this all over again?

But Faye had been so up front with us since the beginning. Our rainbow was almost here, and even all of that fear couldn't stifle the joy and excitement building up inside of me.

It was time.

We went back to the waiting room. In a few minutes, we were going to get to meet him! I think I tried to sit down, but I kept needing to get up—to walk around and pace the room. I felt like one of those cartoon characters that stands in anticipation, chewing their nails into stubs, and vibrating with so much energy that they don't know what to do with it.

And then a nurse walked in holding a beautiful, baby boy.

It had been maybe ten minutes. The longest ten minutes of my life. And there he was, bundled up so tight.

"Cal and Ashley? Would you like to meet your son?"

Hearing those words come out of the nurse's mouth was one of the most amazing experiences I have ever had.

We sat down with him and just stared; we held him in our arms and wondered if this was real. He was so tiny, so amazing, and we were so happy to meet him! The nurse let us have some time with him and we took our first family picture. He was born on December 5th, 2014 at 10:07 p.m. and we named him Mox Parker.

Then we went to the nursery with him. We were back there for a few minutes and one of the nurses said, "You guys were here eight months ago, weren't you?" She remembered us from Kip's adoption. "All of us felt so bad about everything. We were all hurting for you."

The emotion in her face and in her voice brought tears to my eyes. There is something about going through pain and knowing you're not alone that makes everything feel different. Not better, but sometimes it takes the edge off a little bit.

Mox was on the scale. The nurse said they had already weighed him in the surgery room; he was eight pounds, ten ounces, but they were going to check again.

"Oh my, that's how much Kip weighed!" I said.

The nurse weighed him again and got eight pounds, twelve ounces. She looked over at me. "We'll go with the second number!"

After everything was done in the nursery we went to our room and got settled. I sent Faye a text to see how she was doing. She had just had major surgery and I hoped she was doing okay. I told her to let us know when she was ready for us to come to her room.

At around 1:30 a.m. she said she was ready for us. We were still waiting for a nurse to come in and give Mox his first bath and said we would be right down. The nurse took a while to get to us, so we finally made it to Faye's room around 3:30 a.m.

Faye held him and stared at him for a while. She teared up and then cried for a while and at that moment my heart was aching for her. I didn't want her to be hurting.

Nothing about adoption is easy for anyone—on any side of it. We were a grieving couple hoping for a family, feeling joy at finding the child we'd been longing for, for so long. And now Faye would be grieving a loss too. She knew what she wanted. She had made it clear from the start that she thought this was the best plan for the baby—for Mox.

But that didn't mean it wouldn't break her heart to let him go.

We went back to our room to get some rest and said we would come back down when she was ready for us. The next day, Beth came to check on everyone, like she had with Kip.

When she walked in, she said, "Thank goodness you're not in the same room as you were with Kip."

I hadn't even thought of that, but as soon as she said it, I agreed with her. I don't know how I would have handled that.

She stayed for a while and went over some papers we needed to sign. She also went down to Faye's room to check on her before we headed down there again. When we got to Faye's room, we all just hung out and took turns holding Mox. Faye was so respectful of us the whole time. She asked us if we were okay with how things were happening. We tried to be very respectful of her as well—making sure she was getting enough time with Mox. I felt that the hospital stay was going very well.

She eventually asked if any of our family was coming to the hospital. We said no, we didn't think we could have anyone come.

"You guys can do whatever you want," she said. *"He's yours."*

I don't think we realized how badly we needed to hear those words until she said them. I ended up calling my mom to ask her if she would like to come meet Mox. She and my brother Ray hopped in the car right away. When they got to the hospital, I don't think my mom could get in the room fast enough. By the time she got to the bassinet where Mox was and picked him up, tears were streaming down her face. After almost five years of watching us go through so much pain, loss, and waiting—wishing and hoping—all of those feelings that had built up came flooding out.

It was beautiful. It was painful. But mostly, that moment was just full of hope and love.

The next day it was already time for us to leave the hospital. We were so excited to go home and start life with Mox, but my heart was breaking for Faye. I didn't want to leave her there alone. She loved Mox so much and now she had to say goodbye.

We went down to Faye's room for a few hours before we left. Her mom, some friends, and some of the women she worked with at Victoria's Secret were there. Mox had quite the time with all the ladies holding him. It was like a party! I was just happy Faye had so much support around her. Knowing that she would have other people with her as she grieved made my heart feel just a little bit lighter. As I knew very well by now, having people around you doesn't take away the pain—but it does make it easier to manage.

Faye told us we'd better get on the road. She knew we had a long drive. She had shown such amazing care for us by making sure our needs were met throughout this time.

By then it was just her and her mom, us, and Beth. Cal and I started to get Mox hooked up into his car seat, but it was our first time using it so we weren't quite sure what we were doing.

We kind of looked around, looked around again, and then I said, "So . . . we've never done this before. Anyone have any tips?" We all laughed, and Beth helped us out—thank goodness!

Then it was time to say goodbye.

It was difficult to know what emotions to feel—what emotions we *were* feeling—in that moment. Faye had opened her heart and offered the most love any mother could give. I could only imagine how she must have been feeling, but I knew her heart had to be breaking. She had to be in so much pain.

I gave her a long, tearful hug. I don't think I wanted to let go. She gave me the gift that no one else could: the gift of becoming a mother.

I will forever be grateful to her for that.

I told her we would text her when we made it home. It was so surreal to actually leave the hospital with Mox. I sat in the back with him so that I could make sure he was okay during the ride home. I'm pretty sure I just stared at him the whole time. I pinched myself over and over to make sure I wasn't dreaming.

My wish had come true. We had a son! We were a family. He was here—he was with us! I already loved the little guy so much.

When we got home, we introduced Skeeter to him. Cal held Mox as she sniffed his head, probably wondering what this tiny thing was. Skeeter checked him out for a bit and then went back to her usual spot on the couch. I think she got used to him a lot quicker than she'd gotten used to me! The next few days were amazing; we got settled with Mox and started our lives with him. Cal and I took turns getting up with him during the night. He made so many cute noises while he was sleeping.

Mox was born December 5th, and Faye had a court hearing date set for December 10th, which was really quick. I asked Beth if Faye was going to be okay going to court so soon after having major surgery. Beth said she'd be fine to go.

But even though everything was going well, it was still so hard not to think about Faye changing her mind before the hearing. My mind kept replaying the days in the hospital with Kip. I had to keep telling myself: think positively. Don't let those thoughts run through. I had to keep thinking and praying for the best. I only succeeded part of the time.

At around 11:30 a.m. on December 10th, the phone rang. It was Beth. I tried to stay calm, but it was so hard. My stomach had been in knots all morning. No matter how much positive thinking I tried to do, I was still so afraid. I had been through too much pain to *not* feel that fear.

"I am so happy to be the one to call and tell you the news!" Beth said. "We just got done with the court hearing. Congratulations, Berry family!"

Tears of joy and relief streamed down my cheeks and I looked down at Mox. He was really staying with us! I was a *mother*. We were a family.

I asked Beth how Faye was doing. I was also thinking of her at that moment as I held Mox close to my heart. After all the years of disappointment and the very long journey to get to him, it was surreal to have him there and to be the one holding him. After weathering the storms and going through all of that pain with Kip, Mox had shown up for us like our very own rainbow—a picture of hope on the horizon.

I was so excited to tell everyone about Mox Parker, our son!

ORDER IN THE COURT

December 2014 – July 2015

OUR FIRST CHRISTMAS AS A FAMILY THAT year was so very special. We were filled with so much happiness. Holidays can be very hard when you're going through infertility. This time, instead of dreading a family occasion like we had for so many years, we were excited to go.

We would have four months with Mox before we had to start greenhouse season again. I was nervous. It was going to be so hard to leave him during the day and I kept wondering how things would go. It's so easy to get stuck in worries, think ahead too far, and forget to enjoy the present. I think I struggled with that when I would worry about the greenhouse during those months. I had to remind myself to be present with

Mox. I fell more and more in love with him each day, and I didn't want to miss a single moment. I made good use of those blue shoes, the diaper bag, and the onesies I had originally bought for Kip. At first, I thought it would be hard to use them; but since Kip had never worn them, I was okay with Mox using them.

As Mox started to grow, I couldn't believe how many people would say that he looked just like me. I was not expecting that, but it was nice to hear. I think they said that because we both have dark brown eyes—and I felt bad about it sometimes because Faye had really wanted him to have her eye color. Even so, I still definitely see Faye in him.

It was so amazing to do all the motherly things that I had been dreaming about with Mox; but, even after all the years of waiting to be a mother, I knew it wouldn't be all cupcakes and roses. And on top of learning and growing as a new parent, the adoption wouldn't be officially final for another six months.

During that time, the adoption agency sent a social worker once a month for a visit. The social worker came to monitor how things were going in the home, and then we had to hire a lawyer and get a court date to finalize everything legally. We still had that part of the adoption process to go through, and while we were so full of joy as we settled into our family life with Mox, the stress of it loomed in the background. We felt the fear and the worry—like the fear we had felt at the hospital about whether Faye would change her mind—only bigger and more distant somehow.

At least this time it was a little easier to distract ourselves with work. We were a family, we were together, and we wanted to enjoy it as much as we possibly could.

We were also still texting back and forth with Faye. I would send her updates and pictures of Mox, but I struggled with this a lot. I was always overthinking when I should text and when I shouldn't. I wanted to share everything with her, but I didn't want to overshare either. I wanted it to be just the right amount. I never wanted to hurt her by doing too little or too much, and I put a lot of pressure on myself to be perfect.

When Mox was two months old, she came for a visit with a friend of hers. We were happy to have her come—we wanted her to be in our lives as much as she wanted to be—but in the back of my mind I was always hoping she was still okay with everything. Even though the visit went so well, that worry didn't go away. Did she ever regret her decision? Was that visit good for her, or was it hard on her after she left—after she had to say goodbye to Mox again?

I never wanted her to be hurting. I had tried to imagine how she might be feeling over and over again since those days at the hospital, and I could only think of the heartbreak. Did it get easier over time, or did Faye have to keep letting go, again and again, as she let herself grieve?

It wasn't something I wanted to dwell on; but, I couldn't stop myself from thinking about it, especially whenever I texted her updates—and especially leading up to that final court date.

Thankfully, our first greenhouse season with Mox went more smoothly than I expected. We worked things out so that I didn't have to work such long hours and I could be home with him more. We also decided that this summer would be our last season growing vegetables for the farmer's market. We had to split our energy too many ways and it was getting to be too much. If we cut out growing vegetables for the market, then we could put more energy into the greenhouse and the pumpkin patch. And having the summers to spend as a family sounded pretty amazing.

That was also when we got back on track to start building our own house by the greenhouse. The flood four years ago had thrown a wrench into those plans, and now it was so exciting to think we were going to be that close to work. Cal had to check on things often—sometimes heaters broke in the middle of the night and there are plenty of other things that can go wrong—so the convenience of being that close was going to be a big relief.

With all of the projects and plans going on, we were busy. We were finding our rhythm as a family and settling into our life together. But we still had one important day to look forward to—and to worry about.

On July 6th, 2015, we went to court to finalize Mox's adoption.

I was ready for everything to be finalized, but I was also very nervous. We walked up a lot of steps to get to the entrance of the courthouse. We were that many more steps closer to finalizing the adoption. But I still didn't know what to expect. Would it be a big courtroom? Would there be a lot of people there? Our lawyer met us inside, and it was a relief to know we had someone there with us to guide us through the process. He gave us a heads up about some questions the judge might ask.

We got to the courtroom door and had to wait until they called us in. A short while later, a woman came out to let us know they were ready for us. It wasn't a huge room. The only people in the room with us were our lawyer and the lady who I assumed would be taking notes. We waited for a bit longer; then she asked us to rise and the judge walked in. Mox didn't seem to care that we were in court to finalize his adoption. He wanted to get down to crawl and explore this strange new world. Cal and I passed him back and forth and tried to keep him content with some snacks—they always seemed to do the trick.

The lawyer talked for a while, and then the judge had us each come up to the stand to answer some questions; he wanted to know what we did for a living, what kind of home we had, and whether we wanted to adopt this child. It wasn't a long hearing—only about fifteen minutes. Then the judge signed the papers, and it was official! We asked to take a picture with the judge who officially made us a family and then breathed a sigh of relief as we walked out of the courtroom.

I think I was so focused at the time that I didn't even stop to think about how tense I was. I could tell afterwards, though. I went to the bathroom and saw in the mirror that my neck had red blotches all over it. I'd been trying not to be stressed, but I guess that was out of my control. Looking back on it now, there wasn't much to it. The process was fairly simple, and our lawyer was there with us every step of the way. But there's something about being questioned on the stand that just feels so intense. With the officials around—the judge and the lawyer—and the strange stillness of the courtroom; even though we'd done nothing wrong, it almost felt like we were on trial.

But then it was over, and it was done. We stepped out onto the steps of the courthouse and it was suddenly more real than it had ever been. Ever since the nurse in the hospital put Mox in our arms on December 5th, 2014, I had felt like we were officially a family, but having the legal part completed was such a good feeling.

On July 6th, 2015, Mox Parker officially became a Berry!

PCOS

November 2015 – May 2016

I WANTED TO BE THE BEST MOM I COULD BE for Mox. I had fought so hard, for so long, to get to this place: to have my baby boy in my arms. Making sure I was healthy was a huge priority for me. I wanted to know that I was doing everything I could to be the best mother I could be for him.

Also, in the back of my mind, I thought it wouldn't hurt if I could miraculously get pregnant and give Mox a sibling in the next few years.

When Mox was eleven months I started to do more research on PCOS. Ever since my doctor had diagnosed me with it during fertility treatments, PCOS had been a weight on my mind. It doesn't just affect fertility—there's a whole host of other health issues that can arise from PCOS. I wanted to be sure that I was doing everything I could to prevent it from affecting the rest of me—mentally or physically. I bought a book about it and started to do some reading. I thought there might be more information out there for me at that time than there had been when I was first diagnosed in 2012.

When you have PCOS, your hormones are all over the place. Your body produces higher levels of androgens—male hormones that females have in their body, but in lower amounts. With PCOS, you produce too many of them, which causes that extra body hair (or hirsutism) and acne. The symptoms in your body are similar to those felt by people who are prediabetic. I was concerned that if I didn't take control of my symptoms, I would become diabetic later on.

I did a lot of research, and the best solution I found was to focus on keeping symptoms at bay: exercising, eating healthily, and staying away from things that might spike my blood sugar. Exercising helped control my blood sugar levels, so I found that it was good to get up and be active after a meal.

It was frustrating at times. The list of foods to avoid was long. I was having a hard time finding things I *could* eat. I also came across recommendations to stay away from dairy, which was kind of funny to me. When I was first diagnosed, my doctor advised me to keep my weight in check; but he said I could still have a Blizzard from Dairy Queen on the way home from my appointment.

Since I didn't want to deal with mixed messages from all over the place, I decided to get myself a personal trainer. I thought I was in decent shape when I started with her, but I guess I was wrong. The first two weeks with my trainer were so hard to get through. The workouts were intense—so intense I wondered if I would get through them—and I couldn't help wondering if it was all too much for me. Had I made a mistake?

I worked out with her three days a week: Mondays, Wednesdays, and Fridays. I'm glad it wasn't every day. My body needed the days in between to recover. Each workout was fifty minutes long. I was doing High Intensity Interval Training (HIIT), which included weight training with thirty to forty-five seconds of cardio in between sets.

I will never forget, on arm day, we ended a session with twelve pushups, twelve wide pushups, and twelve tricep pushups. Three rounds of pushups! My arms felt like shaky Jello and I pretty much collapsed on the way down on one. My trainer told me that the rep didn't count.

"I can't get my arms to work properly!" I told her. We were laughing, but seriously, I was in pain!

She knew I could do it, though, if I got out of my own head. And she was right. Sometimes, working out is more mental than physical.

After a few weeks I started to feel stronger. The workouts were still hard, but I was able to do them without questioning my chance of survival each time! It was crazy what a few weeks with her and really watching what I ate did, and I was feeling great. I had more energy than I'd had in years—maybe in my whole life—and after three months I was really starting to feel different. It wasn't just the way I felt, either, but the way I thought. As I focused on improving my body, my mindset changed in a positive way. I had more energy, more motivation and drive, and I felt like I could achieve anything I put my mind to.

As I got into the workouts more, I decided I wanted to have a goal to work toward. So, I planned to take fitness pictures of my progress. Since I would probably never get to take maternity pictures (though I was still hopeful that I would get pregnant one day), these would be my "maternity" pictures. I wanted to see how my body would change over the next nine months.

A year went by—an entire year of trying to keep up with my workouts and eating healthy foods. I still wasn't pregnant, but I was definitely feeling better. And having a goal to work toward—one where I could see my progress and improvement along the way—was an amazing boost for my mental health. My PCOS wasn't gone and I hadn't miraculously gotten pregnant, but my hope wasn't gone either. I had the strength to keep fighting.

I was still on the lookout for more options to treat PCOS. At a laser hair removal appointment (one of the ways to treat my symptoms, for which I was very thankful!) the technician and I were making small talk, and I found out that she also had struggled with infertility and PCOS. She asked if I had ever heard of a supplement called Berberine. I hadn't. She told me it was similar to Metformin, which helped keep blood sugar in check. I had been on Metformin for six months in the past, but I never really noticed a change with it. I had stopped taking it after the IVF process failed.

So, I thought, "What the heck. I've tried almost everything now for PCOS. What's one more thing?"

I couldn't believe the results I started seeing after only two weeks. My face felt like butter. It was clear. My acne wasn't out of control at the time, but I was having hormonal breakouts and the Berberine worked like magic. I also noticed a difference around my waist. With PCOS, I tended to hold on to weight around my midsection. I thought I would have abs of steel after all the intense workouts with my trainer—and I did notice a change—but not nearly like what I was expecting. When I took Berberine, it was like the weight melted off my waist. I was so happy with this supplement! Finally, I had found something that helped me in a way that I could actually notice.

But as I had noticed before, my physical health wasn't the only thing that mattered.

All of the grief and pain Cal and I had gone through to get to this point hadn't been magically healed just because we had Mox. The joy of new beginnings doesn't outweigh the heartbreak of loss. If I wanted to be as strong as I could be for Mox, I needed to take care of some of that internal healing as well.

And I found a part of the healing in the most unlikely place.

Around this time, a few of my friends were pregnant. I had dabbled in photography projects from the time I was in college, and my job at the photography studio from back then had taught me a lot. It had been a while since I really did anything like the wedding photography business I'd run on the side, but I still loved taking photos.

I offered to do birth photography for a few of them. I had never done it before, but I was excited to try, and now that I had Mox, the grief that I'd felt when I saw other people growing families of their own wasn't quite so close.

It was so amazing to capture those moments and tell the story of each birthday for those friends in my life. The experience was also a gift to me. I got to be a part of that special time. I had never experienced giving birth, and it was like I got to experience it through those friends, in a way.

I was hooked. Birth photography was my new favorite. And I was on my way to healing in ways I had never imagined were possible.

TRYING — AGAIN

September 2016 – November 2017

B Y THE FALL OF 2016 I REALLY STARTED to think about Mox having a sibling. He was almost two years old, and the break from the adoption process had been good for us.

But Cal didn't want to try again. He thought we had already been through too much. If we wanted to adopt again, we would have to be on a waitlist for six months. Only then would we be able to start the process of renewing our home study.

So, I did what I do best with Cal. I kept talking until I talked him into it.

I wanted to get on that waiting list. Six months was a long time to wait, but I knew Cal wanted Mox to have a sibling. Plus, he made comments every once in a while that he would love a little princess in his life too. After some convincing, I got him on board. I called the adoption agency in September of 2016; our six months would be over the following March.

March—right when greenhouse season starts up. Oops.

I guess I could've timed that a little better! Thankfully when it came time to renew our home study in March, there weren't as many steps as the first time. We just had to do our fingerprints, doctors' appointments, and some paperwork over again. I also had to freshen up our profile book, but I didn't put nearly as much pressure on myself this time. I knew we just needed to be ourselves. That was how a potential family would connect with us.

In the summer of 2017, our book was uploaded to The Village website again. I wasn't as impatient this time. I was so happy with Mox and I felt that if it was meant to be it would happen again. I also had plenty of things keeping me occupied through the summer and well into the fall. While we were wrapping up another pumpkin patch season, my friend Jess and I had started planning a couples' trip. We had both always wanted to stay in a bungalow over the water, so we were planning a trip to Tahiti. The itinerary had a lot of connections, and we had many details to work out.

On the morning of November 2nd, we were finally ready to book our trip. I felt like we had been planning and talking about it for so long. We were finally actually going to go through with it. Jess was busy that morning, so she said we could finalize everything right after lunch.

At around 10 a.m., I got a call from Tenley, our social worker at the time.

"Is Cal home with you?" she asked.

He had gone fishing for the day, so I would have to relay everything to him when he got back.

Tenley told me that there was a young couple who wanted to make an adoption plan. They had picked our family and wanted to meet us. Tenley gave me some background information about the family and proceeded to tell me that the child was a *girl*.

I wasn't expecting to find that out so soon. I couldn't believe how excited I got after she told me. I know I would have been happy if we had another boy, either way I would have been happy, but in the back of my mind all I could think of was how Cal would get his little princess.

Tenley also said that the family had already picked out a name for her: Paislee Rae.

My mind took me a year back to when I was sitting in my living room with my friend, Renee. We had been chatting about kids' names and she said if we ever had a girl, we should name her Paislee.

Had Tenley just said Paislee? I couldn't believe it!

"Think about everything I've told you," Tenley said, to finish up the call. "Get in touch with Cal and see what he thinks. I need an answer by tonight if you want to move forward."

I called Cal right away after I got off the phone with her. He didn't answer. I tried calling again fifteen minutes later and still nothing. I couldn't shake the excitement I'd felt, hearing Tenley say the baby was a girl. It felt like another dream coming true all over again, and I wanted to tell Cal so badly. He must not have had service where he was. I sent about five texts, so that if he did get service again, his phone would really start dinging. Then I called my mom. I had to tell someone. I was just bursting with the news.

Mom was very excited about the possibility of having a granddaughter pretty soon. I also had to call Jess, so I waited until I knew she was available.

"Jess, um . . . so, there's a change of plans. We can't book the vacation. We just got a phone call from Tenley and our family might be growing very soon!"

She took it well. She was excited for us, and I was glad to have her as my friend through what might be another roller coaster of emotions.

About two hours later, Cal finally called me back. I had this immediate sense of relief. I was pretty sure he'd be willing, but I needed his verbal consent before I could call Tenley back, and she'd given us the deadline of that evening.

I picked up the call from Cal and told him everything. He was so excited! He wanted to meet the family. So, the next Wednesday, we drove to meet with Hannah and Derek.

It wasn't our usual four-hour drive. They lived closer—only an hour and forty minutes away. This first meeting was going to be just the four of us. Then we would set up a meeting with Mox, so they could meet him too.

The meeting went well. We did ask early on if we could use Paislee as her middle name. Cal and I both liked the name, but we wanted to name her ourselves. We had other names on our list that we would have loved to use.

Hannah said she would really like her name to be Paislee Rae, though, and I couldn't argue with her. A name is so important and can carry a lot of weight, and they must have picked it out so carefully. We knew we would love Paislee Rae no matter what she was called, so we were okay with letting that go. I did mention to Hannah what my friend Renee had said a year before. They thought that was pretty amazing!

Their social worker, Kay, called us after the meeting and said they were happy and wanted to move forward with the adoption. Hannah was due December 9th, so we had about a month to prepare.

In the meantime, we had a trip to visit some friends planned for the day after we met with Hannah and Derek. We went ahead with the trip anyway. We had just finished the pumpkin patch season, so we wanted the chance to get away and spend some quality time with Mox. It would be our last month as a family of three!

I was taking the trip all in. On the second night, the guys took the boys to a hockey game while my friend Bailey and I went to a "Painting with a Twist" event to have a glass of wine and do some painting. When we walked in, the atmosphere brought a smile to my face. All the canvases were set up already and the paints were portioned out. We each grabbed a glass of wine and headed to the spots marked with our name tags.

I looked at Bailey. "This is going to be fun!" I said.

Everyone was painting the same design under the guidance of the instructor who walked us through it step by step. In between the instructions there was some music playing to liven the mood and we left the event quite proud of the paintings we had created.

Bailey and I stopped for some dessert on the way back. I got a piece of chocolate cake. I let myself have a treat every once in a while, and, boy, was I excited to eat it. After we got home, I was about to take a bite of that delicious-looking cake when my phone rang. It was Kay.

I thought that was weird—she knew we were on vacation—and then I started to worry. Was something wrong? And of course, the biggest concern that ran through my mind was: did Hannah and Derek change their minds?

I picked up and Kay said, "Hannah is in labor!"

My hands started to shake, and my mind just raced. Oh my gosh, we were so far away. It was late at night!

"Should I be trying to get the next flight there?" I asked her. I think I was panicking.

She said no. "Let's wait to see how Hannah progresses."

I didn't want to wait. I knew we needed to be there, and I called Cal right away after talking to Kay. He said we needed to get there too.

My friend Bailey knew we were trying to adopt again. She had asked a little while ago if we'd heard anything and I'd told her no. I said we were still waiting for The Call. I knew that I needed to play things safe to protect myself, but once again I had to come clean—just like I had to with Jess when Mox was born.

I got off the phone with Cal and told Bailey I was sorry but I had kind of fibbed to her the first day of our trip. "We did get picked and she is in labor *right now*!"

I was shaking so badly after I got off the phone, I couldn't take a bite of that cake I had wanted so much. My stomach was in knots. Being this far away was really hard. Cal came back and we decided we were going to get the first flight we could in the morning.

The next morning, it was November 12th, just ten days after we'd received the phone call that Hannah and Derek wanted to meet. Kay called at 8:30 in the morning to give us an update. Paislee was here. She was born at 8:08 a.m.

I couldn't believe we were so far away!

I asked how Hannah was doing and Kay said her delivery went very smoothly. Paislee was out in just a few pushes and Hannah was doing great. We asked if we could get a picture of Paislee and they sent us one. She was just a little peanut, weighing five pounds, seven ounces.

We couldn't wait to meet her. We got the earliest flight we could, but still didn't arrive until late that night. As soon as we landed and got checked into our hotel, I went to get a few things at the store. I got some flowers to bring for Hannah and Derek the next morning.

It was so hard to sleep that night. Kay had said to text Hannah in the morning to let them know when we would be on our way. We went up to the hospital at 8:30 the next morning. When we got there, Hannah and Derek were very emotional. They were so young. Except for Kay, it had been just the two of them at the hospital the whole time. I was excited to meet Paislee and hold her for the first time, but it was hard to be happy and excited. Adoption is never easy, and I knew they were hurting. Just as with Faye and Kara, I could sense that heartbreak from a mile away.

We hung out in their room for a while, and Cal and I both got to hold Paislee for the first time. She was so tiny and so very chill. She hardly ever cried.

Derek said, "I wonder if she'll always be like this."

How often would he wonder things about Paislee after he had to say goodbye? I couldn't bear to think about it.

We told them that we would give them some time alone again with Paislee. The nurse took us to the room we would be staying in just down the hall and about a half hour later Hannah sent me a text. She asked if they could bring Paislee over to our room. I said of course, and I heard them when they started coming down the hall.

Hannah was crying very hard. When they got to the room, she said it was too hard to have Paislee with them. I asked Hannah if I could give her a hug. She said yes and I did. Just like with Faye, I wanted so badly to take her under my wing and take her pain away. They were going through so much sorrow and grief, and they didn't have anyone there with them to support them.

As I was hugging her, I said, "Paislee is so very loved already."

I don't know if it was comforting. I hoped it was. There wasn't much more to say, and they went back to their room while we spent some time alone with Paislee. Mox was with my mom at a hotel nearby and Cal went to get him so he could meet his sister. He was somewhat interested in her for a second and then he went on to the next thing to explore. Two years old—you've got to keep things interesting.

That night Paislee had some tests done to make sure she was ready to go home the next day. She had a car seat test at 2:30 a.m. They needed to monitor her in the car seat for the same amount of time she would be in the car. Since she was so tiny, they had to make sure she would be okay to ride the whole time.

Paislee passed all of her tests and was ready to go home the next day. Cal brought Mox up again the next morning so we could all be together for a while before we left. Hannah and Derek wanted to meet Mox and see us all as a family. Kay also joined us to make sure everything was going smoothly before we left.

When it was time to say goodbye and get on the road, Kay asked how Hannah and Derek would like to leave the hospital. They said that we should go first and they would leave a little bit after us. They both were being really strong that day. It was still hard to say goodbye. But everything went well as we were getting ready to leave.

Before we could head home, we had to stop by the hotel where my mom had been staying with Mox. We went into the room so my mom could meet Paislee quickly and then we would get on the road to head home. Paislee was in the car seat in the hotel room and Mox sat beside her.

He looked at her. "Hi, Paissee," he said.

I said, "Is that your baby sister?"

"Yeaaah!" Mox said. Then added, "Hey Mama, hey Dada, you dottt Paissee?"

We all laughed, and Cal said, "Yes, we got Paissee."

No one wanted to correct him with "Yes, we adopted Paislee." It was such a cute moment.

We got on the road to head home and start our life as a family of four; we were feeling so very thankful to be blessed with a son, and now a daughter. The Berry family was complete.

PAISLEE RAE

November 2017

WE TOLD A FEW FAMILY AND FRIENDS Paislee was at home with us, but we wanted to wait to tell anyone else until Hannah and Derek went to their court hearing. We were all doing well, Paislee was still so chill, and she still hardly ever cried. We had to set alarms throughout the night to get up and feed her. The doctors said we should make sure she was eating every two to three hours.

We tried to get used to life as a family of four. We made sure Mox was always getting attention from one of us because we knew that having a sibling might make him feel left out. We made sure we were aware of that, and it turned out Mox loved having a baby sister. He would read to her by the mamaRoo and he liked it when she would watch him play hockey.

On our third day home, I took Paislee to her first checkup. She was doing great. She was the same weight as when we left the hospital. The doctor looked her over, checked her heart and her temperature, and everything was normal.

Three nights later, on November 19th, I set my alarm to get up for her next feeding at 3:00 a.m. When it was time, I got the bottle ready and tried to feed her, but she wasn't interested. She didn't want it. I thought that was strange. She only ate a few ounces at a time, but she would still always eat.

I woke Cal up. He was the one who fed her last. I told him Paislee wouldn't eat. He said she ate a lot from the last bottle, so maybe she wasn't hungry. A few hours later, Cal got up and tried to feed her again. He noticed something was on her cheek. He turned the light on. It was blood.

"Ashley, something's wrong. Paislee's not looking good."

I got up to check on her. Her color wasn't good, and I started to shake. I felt sick to my stomach. What was happening?

I called the ambulance. While I was on the phone with dispatch, I was running around frantically, trying to get my clothes on so we could leave as soon as they arrived. I'd never had to call 911 before. After I got off the phone, I called June right away. She was the closest one to us. I told her Cal and I needed to take Paislee to the hospital.

"Can you come here and be with Mox until my mom can get here?"

Mox was still sleeping, which I was thankful for. I didn't want anything to scare him.

As soon as the paramedics arrived, they put Paislee on oxygen. She instantly regained some color. The paramedics said it would be best if we followed the ambulance in our car. Paislee was in her car seat and I didn't want to leave her. I wanted one of us to ride with her. But we followed right behind, making sure the ambulance was in sight the whole time.

On the way to the hospital, we called Kay to let her know what was happening. She told us she'd be seeing Hannah and Derek that night. "I'll tell them what's happening when you know more. Call me."

When we arrived at the ER, they brought us to a room right away and laid Paislee on a big bed with the oxygen right beside her. I felt like things were moving so slowly. We were probably there for only two minutes, but it felt like twenty to me. She started sounding like she couldn't breathe.

I ran out into the hallway to get someone. "Someone needs to come in here!"

No one had come in to talk to us yet. I think they were trying to go over her symptoms, but in the moment, it felt like nothing was being done. I felt like they needed to be trying to do something right away—trying to make her better.

The nurses that came in said they needed to try to get some blood from her to see what was happening so they could diagnose her, but they couldn't get any because she was so tiny. They tried a few different times. After about twenty minutes, they finally called a neonatal nurse practitioner. She got blood from Paislee right away without any trouble and then left just as quickly.

Everything still felt so slow to me. I don't know how much time passed as we waited. I was reeling. I think I was in shock and at the same time, Cal and I were trying to comfort each other. We tried to believe that it would be okay. We were at the hospital and they were helping her. They were going to help Paislee.

At some point, a doctor came to talk to us. "We think she may have an infection in her blood. Sepsis. But we won't know for sure until the cultures come back from the lab."

We waited and waited some more and then they said they wanted to transfer Paislee to the neonatal intensive care unit (NICU).

They sat me in a wheelchair so I could hold her all the way there. Then they took her into a smaller room. We couldn't be in the room with her right away. There were about six nurses around Paislee and they were working very fast to get her all hooked up. We needed to be out of the way. They were going to intubate her. Since her umbilical cord hadn't dried up yet, they were able to hook up the lines to put all of the medicine and fluid through there. I was thankful that she didn't have to be poked anymore.

We watched from a distance, praying that they would save Paislee's life. I finally felt like something was actually being done to save her, and even though it was hard, I stayed back and let them work.

We were sitting across the hall waiting when a nurse came to ask if she could get us anything. I was so sick to my stomach; I didn't want to eat or drink. But I knew I had to try—we hadn't eaten since the night before. The nurse brought us some food and I tried to force down a few bites. I don't even remember what the food was. I just wanted to wake up from the nightmare.

The doctor that I had seen a few days before came up to the NICU. He thought Paislee had a bacterial infection called group B Strep. It could be treated with antibiotics, so he started her on them right away. They began some more tests to learn more about what was happening, and once they had her all hooked up, we were allowed to go back in and be with her; but first we had to get all suited up in gowns to protect her. Once we were in the room, we just sat beside her, praying that she would get the help she needed, and the antibiotics would fight off the infection.

There was a fast beeping noise and one of Paislee's arms went stiff. One of her legs did the same. The nurse rushed in. She said Paislee was having a seizure. After it had passed, the nurse said she was having them due to the infection. I felt so helpless. I wanted to do something to make her better. It was so hard to see her go through this. I felt like I could hardly breathe. The seizures continued about every twenty minutes and my heart kept breaking. She was so tiny, so innocent, and in so much pain.

That evening, Paislee stabilized. So, at around eight o'clock, Cal decided to go home to be with Mox. My mom and brothers were there, but we wanted one of us to go home each night to be there with him and one of us to always stay with Paislee.

At around 10:45 p.m. I went out to the chair across the hall to rest my eyes for a bit—Paislee's room only had a hard rocking chair and a desk chair. The nurse brought me a blanket and said she would come get me if she needed to. I had only closed my eyes for a few minutes when I heard some commotion. I looked over and some nurses were in Paislee's room. The nurse from before came out and got me.

"Paislee has had a really bad seizure; this time it caused her to stop breathing for a little while, but she's stable again."

I started to get pretty emotional. I was delirious from not getting any sleep and it was so hard for me to wrap my head around what was happening. I remember praying, "God, please don't take her away. Let her fight this infection. Help her to get better." I couldn't stop sobbing. There was nothing I could do, and I was so worried. Our family was together, complete after all this time. How could we lose her like this?

I didn't want to say goodbye.

The nurse said, "I would call your husband and tell him to come. Would you like me to get the pastor here to baptize her?"

I said yes. I tried calling Cal, but he didn't pick up. I found out later that he was in such a deep sleep he didn't hear his phone.

At 11:30 p.m. the pastor came to baptize Paislee; I sat by her bassinet and she held on to my finger. This wasn't how it was supposed to happen. We were supposed to do this at the church in my hometown, like we had with Mox. I was going to find her a beautiful lace dress to wear. It was going to be a happy time with family and friends, not one where I was fighting to see through my tears.

I was sobbing uncontrollably. I prayed so hard that she would get better. That she would fight this. Eventually, I called my mom and asked her if she could come to be with me and Paislee. We were only permitted to have one grandparent come—no one else was allowed. Mom ended up arriving at around 4:30 in the morning and I met her where she checked in. I talked with her as she got suited up and washed her hands for the mandatory five minutes.

While we were talking, she started to cry. "Why her? Why is this happening to a tiny, innocent baby?"

Hadn't I been asking myself the same thing all this time?

"We just have to keep praying Mom," I said. I couldn't bring myself to say anything else. I was sure I'd fall apart again.

Paislee was stable after the scare we had earlier that night. Mom stayed with me until the morning of the 21st, and at 6:30 a.m. she went back home so Cal could come to be with Paislee.

It was another long day of waiting and praying she would improve. Every ten minutes, they would bring something in for her and check on her. They were giving her platelets and seizure medication. It seemed to help, since she wasn't having the seizures as often.

She was very sick. We found out it was late-onset group A Strep. The symptoms are very similar to group B Strep, and it can lay dormant until around seven to ten days after birth. They found the infection in her spinal fluid, so she had meningitis, but it was in her blood too, so she had sepsis. It was also in her lungs, so she had pneumonia. It had taken over her tiny body so quickly.

More test results came back, and she was showing signs of fighting the infection. So, there was hope. The doctor estimated she would be in the hospital for about two weeks.

The whole time this was happening, we kept Hannah and Derek updated. They were very concerned. I had the nurse call them directly and tell them about everything that was going on with Paislee, and on November 22nd, Hannah came to be with us and Paislee at the hospital for about three hours. It was nice to have her there with us. We were all scared. We all loved Paislee very much and having all that love surrounding her was amazing. When Hannah left again and went back home, she told us to keep her updated.

That night, I left and Cal stayed with Paislee. I went home to be with Mox, to sleep a bit, and to shower. The next morning was Thanksgiving Day.

I played with Mox for a while. My mom was going to make a little Thanksgiving dinner so I could eat before I went back to the hospital; Cal came home around 11:00 a.m. to eat and shower quickly. He said they had taken Paislee down for an MRI to see if any of the infection had caused long term effects.

It was so hard. When I left the hospital, I felt like I needed to be back there and when I left Mox, I felt like I needed to be with him. My heart was tearing me in two. I knew Mox was having a blast with my family and I think I was also glad that he was protected from all of the fear and stress, but it was hard to be away from him. This was not how our Thanksgiving was supposed to be.

We ate quickly and made our way back to the hospital. We wanted to be there when Paislee got back to the room. We made it just as they were bringing her back and got suited up to sit in the room with her. We weren't there long before the doctor walked in. She said she had the MRI results—I didn't realize they would have them so soon.

The doctor showed us the scan. I could tell when I looked that it wasn't good. She said Paislee had suffered severe strokes as a result of the infection.

"I am so very sorry, but *if* she survives, she will not have a high quality of life. She won't be able to leave this hospital bed."

I felt like the world was pulled out from under me. My stomach twisted and dropped, and I couldn't get myself to stop shaking. We thought she was improving. We thought we were going to bring her back home. We were a family of four and this was not happening.

It couldn't be happening.

"You can keep her on life support, or you can take her off—it's your choice," the doctor said. "Talk about it with Hannah and Derek."

I thought it had been hard to breathe before, but now I felt like I was drowning. How could we do that to Hannah and Derek? How were we supposed to make that call to tell them? They had just said goodbye to her. After everything they'd been through, how were they supposed to say goodbye again?

It was so hard to move and breathe, let alone think. At 2:36 p.m., Hannah called us on a group call, so that Derek could join. I let Cal talk. I couldn't bring myself to say anything. He started to tell them what the doctor had said; he got about halfway through and couldn't talk anymore.

I took over and tried to tell them. We were all sobbing over the phone. We agreed that we didn't want Paislee to be in pain anymore, and that the best thing for her was to take her off life support. Hannah and Derek said they would be there in about two to three hours. We got off the phone; a nurse had been in the room with us for the phone call.

She said, "I am so very sorry. That was the most painful phone call I've ever heard."

She might have been crying too.

The NICU said we could have one or two people come while we waited for Hannah and Derek to get there so I called my mom.

"Mom, Paislee isn't going to make it. We have to let her go."

She began to cry. "Oh, Ashley. . . I am so very sorry . . . I am so very sorry, Ashley."

"If you'd like to come say goodbye to her, you can."

Cal called Breanna next to tell her and ask if she would like to come. Then the doctor came back in and went over some things while we waited. What Cal said next was so hard to think about.

"I don't want her to be gasping for air after we take her breathing tube out."

I hadn't even let my mind go there, but once he said it, it was all I could think about. She was already in so much pain. She was so small and going through so much. If there was anything we could do to lessen her suffering, we wanted to do that.

The doctor said, "I'm sorry, but it may happen. That is the body's natural reaction. We're going to do everything we can to make her as comfortable as possible."

It was all we could ask for.

While we waited for everyone, the nurse came in to change Paislee's bedding and diaper. She asked if I would hold Paislee while she changed the bedding. So, I held up our little princess and stared at her. I tried to keep myself composed. She was not the same Paislee we had brought home eleven days ago. She was swollen and her skin was very purple. When I looked at her, I knew it was time to let her go. As much as my heart ached in the moment—and will always ache when I think of it—I knew we were making the right choice for her.

My mom and brother Ray arrived at the hospital, and I could hear them coming down the hall. Ray was sobbing, and as soon as he walked into the room, he wrapped me in a hug and cried on my shoulder for a while. We all just stared at Paislee in disbelief. I kept asking myself, "How can this be happening?" but of course, no one could answer that for me.

Breanna arrived shortly after and they all stayed for about forty-five minutes. There wasn't much anyone could say or do. It was just nice to have a few people with us for a little while, as we waited for Hannah and Derek to arrive.

At around 6:00 p.m., Hannah texted, "We're here. Do we go to the same spot?"

They met us in the same room we had been in for the last four days. We all spent some time with Paislee and then the nurses said when we were ready, they would take us to a room where we could all have more space and be more comfortable.

The doctor was in the room with us for a while. She said something I think we all needed to hear, even if maybe we weren't ready to receive it in that moment. She looked at Hannah and Derek and then she looked over at Cal and me.

"You need to know that this is not any of your faults," she said. "Paislee got very sick, very fast, and there was nothing anyone could've done."

I don't know if there's any way to stop the questioning or the blaming—the wondering, "Where did I go wrong?" But the heart of the doctor's words has since soothed something desperate inside of me, and I don't know how much harder this all might have been without those words.

And it was still hard. It still *is* hard. It was agony like nothing I've ever felt before, or since.

When we got to the larger room where we were going to say goodbye to Paislee, we asked if they could wait to take out her breathing tube until we had all said our goodbyes. The doctor had to give her oxygen manually, by squeezing the oxygen bag every few seconds until it was time. There wasn't a dry eye in that room. The doctors and nurses were crying. One of the nurses even got us all Tylenol. Everyone had headaches from crying so hard for so long.

When it was my turn to hold Paislee and say goodbye, I looked down at her tiny face. It brought me back to when my grandpa had passed away. I was in the room with him and the hour before he passed his eyes were moving behind his eyelids like he was seeing things. Maybe it was a bright light? It was almost like he was already gone, but his body was still hanging on, waiting to take that last breath.

Paislee had that same look. There's nothing anyone can say or do at that moment, but I hoped she was seeing the same thing my grandpa had seen. I hoped she was filled with peace and so much love and happiness.

I whispered to her as I held her. I told her how excited I was when I found out she was a girl and how much I was going to miss her. I told her that I loved her. I told her it was okay for her to go now and that she didn't have to be in pain anymore.

I was the last one to hold Paislee. And then it was time.

The doctor came over and took the breathing tube out. I held Paislee tight and close. Hannah knelt down in front of me and put her hand on her. Cal was standing behind me and Derek was on the other side of me. Paislee was surrounded by so much love. She had all four of her parents there with her.

A few moments after the tube was out, she took the tiniest breath. It wasn't a gasp. It was one tiny breath, so small and so innocent, just like her. In that moment, seeing that she didn't fight for air, that she was peaceful and calm, I knew we had all made the right decision.

The doctors turned off the heart monitor so we wouldn't hear it beeping. They said her heart might still beat for a while. It was made to beat for a hundred years and it was still very strong.

We all took turns holding her again, making sure we kept telling her we loved her. And after forty minutes, we started to see the color leave Paislee's face. The doctor checked her heart.

She was gone.

She was now our beautiful guardian angel in heaven.

SAYING GOODBYE

November 29th, 2017

Paislee Rae,

You were our little Kadupul—our "flower from heaven"—one of the rarest and most valuable flowers in the world. So beautiful and fragrant, most will never get to see one. It blooms at midnight and is done before dawn. We don't really know why some of the most beautiful and precious things are only here for a short time. Our little Paislee, you were loved and touched by many, you'll remain in our hearts forever.

— From your great aunt

The next day, all four of us planned Paislee's funeral together. It was comforting that we all had each other. Kay and Tenley joined us to support us and make sure everything went smoothly. The Village Family Service Center also helped with some of the funeral costs.

At the funeral home, we picked out the tiniest white casket. It was only fifteen inches long. We went to the flower shop to pick out bouquets for the funeral. I wanted them to be big round balls and told the florist I didn't want them to look like funeral flowers. Everyone liked yellow so we went with some yellow and white flowers: roses, lilies, and hydrangeas. We wanted everything to be perfect for Paislee.

Back at our house, we picked out the songs we were going to play at her funeral: Sarah McLachlan's "Angel" and "I Will Remember You." We also asked Hannah and Derek if we could hyphenate her last name on her headstone, since they had not gone to court yet. They said that would be okay.

At the end of that day I just kept thinking, "Did we just do this?"

"Did we just plan a funeral?"

"Did we just pick out a tiny, white casket?"

"This isn't real . . . it just can't be real."

It was so hard to wrap my head around everything. I had so many questions, but the biggest one was *why*? Why did this happen to an innocent little baby? Was there something we could've done? Should I have seen the signs earlier? I kept going back to when the doctor had told us there was nothing we could have done.

"You need to know that this is not any of your faults. Paislee got very sick, very fast, and there was nothing anyone could've done."

Even though we had all needed to hear those words, they still hadn't sunk in. It was hard—so hard—to not think that there was something we could have done to save her. Hannah and Derek had picked us to protect her. I was her Mom. I was supposed to protect her, and I felt like I had failed.

We had tried to keep Mox's life as normal as possible during Paislee's illness. He had been busy with my family and Cal's family while we were at the hospital. They took him bowling and he played with his cousins. He was too young to understand what was going on. I knew I was going to have to tell him, but I was trying to find the right way.

The next day, Mox and I were at the house and I said, "Mox, come over here."

I was standing by our sliding glass window, looking at the sky. I pointed up. "Paislee lives up in heaven now. She's an angel."

He said, "Oh. Okay."

I knew he probably still didn't understand. He was only two years old. But I wanted to make sure he knew what was going on. The last thing I wanted was for him to be confused, to start asking where Paislee had gone, and why she couldn't be at home with us. I think that would have shattered whatever was left of my heart at the time.

The day of Paislee's funeral came and I didn't want to go. I didn't want it to be real. I still couldn't bring myself to believe that this was actually happening. But somehow, I was also very strong that day. I wasn't trying to be. I don't know if I just didn't have any tears left in me, but I think I only shed a few small tears at that point. I knew Paislee wasn't there anymore. I had already said goodbye to her at the hospital.

The grief that I was experiencing at that time was different than with Kip, but it's hard to explain how it was different. With Kip I think I had felt it could still change. He was out there, growing and living in the world, and he could come back to us one day. But with Paislee, it all happened so fast. We got the call that Hannah was in labor on November 11th and Paislee's funeral was on November 29th. Maybe I was still in shock, but I knew we made the best decision for her. She was at peace, so I think that somehow filled my own heart with peace, even though I was hurting.

I was definitely still grieving. It felt like a part of my heart was permanently missing from my chest. But I was much stronger after Paislee. I wanted to be strong for my family, and for Hannah and Derek, so I went to that funeral and put our baby girl to rest knowing she would always be a part of me, no matter what.

ONE MORE TRY

May - August 2018

THE MONTHS PASSED BY AND WE WERE back in greenhouse season. I was ready to go back to work. It was one of the things that helped Cal and me stay grounded. Ever since we started the journey to our family, the greenhouse had been a constant in our lives. It kept our minds occupied and kept us moving forward. After we lost Kip, we came home and Cal went right back to work. And once I was ready, I did too.

It was like that with Paislee, too. I think it was a kind of release for us both. The only problem was that, when I water, I think a lot. On Mother's Day in 2018, I was doing my watering before we opened to customers for the day. I was in the back all by myself. I started to think about Paislee and how I missed her. Why had everything happened the way it did?

I was so thankful for Mox. He was at home and healthy and he made my heart so full, but a piece of my heart was also missing. That Mother's Day, I began to cry and just let it all come out. Cal's mom Lynn happened to walk by; she noticed I was crying and came up to me and gave me a big hug. She didn't say anything. No words needed to be said. She knew why I was crying. She just wanted to be there for me and give me that hug—a hug that I very much appreciated.

I think that moment of grief also triggered something in me. I started to get back into the mindset I had when Mox was eleven months old. I wanted to try to fix my eggs. I wanted to try to get pregnant naturally again.

I convinced myself that I could do it, too. I could eat all the right foods and take the right supplements and it would happen.

I wanted to get a hormone panel test to see if things had changed over the years or if they were still all over the place. I got some blood work done first. When the results came in, the doctor wanted me to try to change a few things before I took the hormone panel test. She wanted me to go on the

Paleo diet for eight weeks, so I did. It was not easy to get through the greenhouse season on that diet. There wasn't much I could eat, and I was walking about 25,000 steps a day. I needed a lot of calories to keep my energy levels up, so I would have a snack every fifteen minutes—raw cashews, Larabars, more cashews. There wasn't much to choose from when I was at the greenhouse every day.

I stuck to the diet. I was really proud of myself. After eight weeks, I did the hormone test and I was so excited to see how my progress had affected my body. I had to spit in a cup ten days out of my cycle and freeze it until I was ready to send the samples in. Then I had to wait—again—for the results.

They did not turn out as I had hoped. At a follow-up appointment, my doctor told me, "You definitely have PCOS, and a hormonal PCOS, not an insulin PCOS. Your progesterone levels are very low—they have almost flatlined." And then she added, "I don't think you even ovulated this month."

This was normal with PCOS. They're called anovulatory cycles: you still seem to have a normal cycle, but due to the insufficient levels of progesterone, no egg is released. They can still cause heavy bleeding and are easily mistaken for a real period.

She also told me that my testosterone levels (androgens) were still very high.

I was defeated again. After everything I had done, after trying so hard, I thought for sure I could regulate my hormones. I wanted so badly to experience the feeling of life moving and growing inside of me—to feel that close bond that I had seen with so many mothers around me. And it hadn't worked.

I threw myself into the greenhouse work again—that cycle of working and thinking too much. Then July came around and we had some time off. I was preparing for the pumpkin patch. We had decided we wanted to have a Paislee Rae Day in her memory and we would donate money from the day to the Angel Fund, which would be used for birth families and adoptive couples who came across unexpected expenses. The Village was so amazing to all of us during the adoption and loss of Paislee and we wanted to give back in whatever way we could.

Our adoption profile book was still on The Village website. I happened to be looking on the website one day. I still wanted Mox to grow up with a sibling and I still wanted to fight for our family. I happened to see a notice about embryo adoption, so I looked into that next.

The process is pretty much exactly how it sounds. With embryo adoption, you adopt embryos from a couple who has completed their family and have embryos left over. If we were to do embryo adoption it would be like adoption, but I would get to experience pregnancy as well. The idea took over. The more I thought about it, the more I wanted to try it. So, I talked to Cal and convinced him we should explore the option.

I called a fertility clinic that does embryo adoption and set up a meeting with the doctor. I had to have all of our IVF records transferred over to the new clinic so he could go over our past history. The meeting was scheduled for July 13th. The doctor and I were talking, and I brought up the embryo adoption process.

"I'm confused," the doctor suddenly said. "Why are we not using your eggs and your husband's sample?"

I didn't answer for a few seconds. Now I was the one who was confused. What was that supposed to mean?

"Are you looking at my previous ultra-sounds?" I asked. "They said something was wrong with my eggs. They didn't have any more tests they could do."

"You have PCOS. Research has come a long way since you first were diagnosed," he said. "You guys only tried IVF once. You need to give it at least three tries."

He was very confident that I could get pregnant through IVF from what he had seen. My mind was blown. Now I had to rethink everything. The hope that I could get pregnant was so tantalizing. Just like with embryo adoption, the more I thought about it, the more the idea grew on me. It was something I had wanted so badly, for so long. I had been wanting it all along—throughout the adoption process—even though I didn't believe it was possible. But now this doctor was telling me it was. It *could* be.

If we were going to do IVF again, we would have to make an appointment in the next month. I had to make a decision. I prayed and asked God to send me a sign. It's always a struggle to know what to do and what to try. Were we supposed to try IVF again? Were we supposed to stay on the adoption list and continue to wait for The Call? I wanted to do what was right. *Tell me what to do! What's our plan?*

I called Cal and we talked about it. He was definitely hesitant. He didn't know if we should try IVF again after what we had already been through. There was nothing easy about the process. It wasn't a simple test or procedure—it was a series of scheduled, exhausting steps with no guarantee at the end. But I did what I do best with Cal. I talked him into it. I didn't have my sign from God, but maybe I didn't need one this time. We made our decision together. I went ahead and made the appointment. We were ready to get this process started again!

An hour later, my phone rang.

"Hi, Ashley!" It was Tenley. "Is Cal with you?"

How many times had I heard that question now? He wasn't, so I called him home and we called Tenley back together.

"I have a birth mother who wants to make an adoption plan," Tenley said.

I couldn't believe what I was hearing. We had just decided to go through with IVF! What were we supposed to do now?

Tenley told us about the birth mother and that it was a very high-risk pregnancy. She mentioned that the mother had epilepsy and had experienced a few bad seizures while pregnant. "I want to know if you guys would like us to put your book in for her to pick from. Think about it for a while and get back to me."

We got off the phone and my first thought was about what I had prayed for just a few hours earlier. I had asked God for a sign—something unbelievable, miraculous, and entirely coincidental. I asked for something to help me make up my mind. We got that surprise call from our social worker shortly after we made the decision to try IVF again. How could it be anything else but the sign I had asked for?

Knowing that the pregnancy was so high risk was a little scary to think about. After all we'd been through, after losing Paislee, I didn't know how much more I could handle. And there was Mox. He was still young, but he was getting older. Would he be able to understand what was going on?

But at the same time, there was this sense of peace that flooded over me. I felt like it was all going to be okay. Everything just felt *right*.

We did some research on epilepsy after we got off the phone. Cal and I talked it through. Together, we made the decision to tell Tenley that we would like our book to be put in. We called her back to let her know.

"Okay, well now that I know your decision on that, I have something to tell you."

We both took a deep breath. What now?

"She hasn't selected a book yet, but she has already looked at your book many times online. She's very serious about your family. It's not for sure yet, but she'll be coming in on Wednesday to make her selection."

That was definitely not what we had expected to hear. As she talked, and afterward, I had to try to not get too excited. I had to manage my expectations again to avoid getting my hopes too high. *If it happens, it happens*, I decided. If not, we could proceed with IVF.

The next Wednesday I headed back home after lunch with a friend. I got closer to our house and saw Cal and Tenley standing in the driveway. That made me nervous. Why show up in person? Why hadn't she called us to tell us what she needed to say?

Did the birth mother not pick our family? Maybe Tenley just wanted to be there for us because she knew how much we had suffered already.

I got out of my car and my stomach was doing flips.

"After all you have been through, I wanted to come and tell you in person that she has picked you guys!" Tenley said.

I could have collapsed in relief. "I was so nervous that you came in person! I didn't know what to expect," I told her. It was like I didn't know whether to laugh or cry. I was so relieved.

Tenley smiled. "I just wanted to see the look on your faces. After everything you've been through, I'm sharing in your joy. Let's set up a time when you guys can go and meet with Mira."

We set up a meeting for the following Monday, July 23rd. I asked Tenley if she knew the gender and she said no. Mira wanted to be the one to tell us. Mira was excited about all the outdoor things our family did. Tenley did tell us that the birth father was killed in a car accident about halfway through Mira's pregnancy.

"Mira's excited for the baby to be able to go hunting and fishing with Cal!" Tenley said.

After Tenley left, Cal and I both said we thought it was a boy. It wasn't that either of us believed a girl couldn't go fishing and hunting, but that was the way the comment sounded to us. After losing Paislee, we were both hoping for another girl—just like after we lost Kip we were hoping for a boy. But we knew we would be very happy and thankful if it was a boy too. We still wouldn't know for sure until our meeting with Mira.

I cancelled the IVF appointment and, that Monday, we set out on that same four-hour drive we had been on before. Mira lived in the same town as Kara and Faye.

When we got to The Village for our meeting, Mira and her stepmother Jan were already in the room waiting for us. We introduced ourselves and started to talk and get to know one another. Mira told us about her pregnancy and how it had been going. We told her more about the greenhouse, the pumpkin patch, and our life with Mox.

Then, Mira let it slip. She was talking about the baby and she said "her." She hadn't officially told us the gender yet.

"Oops!" she said. "Well, that is not how I was going to tell you, but it's a girl!"

I was so excited, tears streamed down my face. We didn't tell Mira about Paislee at that meeting—I don't know if I was scared she might change her mind or if it would be too painful to tell her, but I just couldn't find the words. We would see Mira again in about three weeks, so we decided to tell her then. I could still hardly believe this was all happening.

Mira was due on September 9th, 2018. We had about seven weeks to wait. This time I wanted to tell a few of my close friends. I knew that it could still possibly change like it had with Kip, but I wanted to go through the excitement of telling a few people. When someone is pregnant, they get to announce their pregnancy and do a gender reveal if they want. But with adoption, nothing is final until after the baby is born. It's hard to announce it and get excited. We had been through this a couple of times, so we knew what oversharing looked like. But I still wanted to feel some of that excitement and anticipation for myself.

I let myself tell a few people and enjoy the moment and then I just tried to soak up our last weeks as a family of three. We took Mox on a family trip, treated him to lunch dates, and just enjoyed being with him like we always had. We were just more conscious of it during that time.

On the way to our family trip, we set up another meeting with Mira. I was excited to see her again and talk with her. It's always nice to get to know the birth family as much as possible before the baby is born. I told her about what happened with Paislee and about the special day we were planning at our pumpkin patch in her memory.

Later that same night, Mira's social worker, Joy, called to talk for a bit. I was nervous in a way. What if my conversation with Mira about Paislee had affected our relationship? What if she'd changed her mind?

But what Joy said took all that worry away. "Mira can't believe that happened to you. She wants to give you this gift even more now. It was so very good to hear that and she was very happy with the way things were going. She said it was nice being able to get together again."

It was incredible to see everything fall into place this time. As always, the mix of emotions was still there. The fear, excitement, worry, and anticipation. But after such a hard, painful season, the hope we found with Mira started to feel like a brand-new chapter in our lives. I had been hoping for another rainbow, and I felt like I was just starting to see the colors.

ONE MORE RAINBOW

August - September 2018

THERE WAS ONE MORE PIECE OF A difficult life chapter we still had to close. For the last three months, Skeeter had been in a lot of pain. She had a big bump on her hip. I had taken her to the vet to get her a checkup and they did an x-ray. She had terrible arthritis. They said she was thirteen years old and there wasn't much they could do for her.

They prescribed pain medication for Skeeter, but she was still suffering—and it was hard to see. She had been there with us through everything. From the time Cal and I first met, to being at the greenhouse every day, to starting the journey to our family, Skeeter was always there and happy to see us no matter what, and I didn't want this to be the end. I had been dreading this moment for so many years. I wanted her to always be there with us; and even though I knew it would happen eventually, I never wanted the time to come. I think I was dreading having to say another hard goodbye.

She had been limping on one leg for a while and by August 21st, 2018, she couldn't walk on that leg at all anymore. We could tell the pain medication wasn't helping. I was hoping she would go on her own. That night she was panting and in so much pain, she seemed delirious. She wanted to go outside at 3:30 in the morning. I was hoping she would let go then. I hung out with her by the door in my pajamas and stroked her fur.

"You can go now girl; you've lived a great life. You've lived the best life a dog could live."

She laid out there for an hour at the bottom of the hill and I just watched her. But she didn't go. She hopped back to the sliding glass door and wanted back in.

On August 22nd, we finally said goodbye. She had been part of our family from the very start, and even though I wasn't sure that she liked me at first, we'd grown on each other over time. And she had been so good with Mox.

The day we said goodbye to Skeeter was one of the hardest days, but I found comfort in the idea that she would get to see Paislee again. Somewhere out there, I felt the two of them would be looking down on us—our sweet girls, keeping an eye on us from somewhere over the rainbow. I think it helped to have Mira's delivery to look forward to during the grief. It gave my thoughts some direction on the days when I always seemed to be thinking too much.

At one of Mira's appointments, they found out that the baby was breech. In order for Mira to have a natural delivery, the baby's head was supposed to be down, but her feet were down instead. If she didn't turn on her own in the womb, the doctors would have to try to turn her manually. They attempted this one week before Mira's due date. Jan was the one who called to update me.

"They had no luck turning the baby," Jan said. "She even kicked the doctor a few times while she was trying to turn her. Seems she has her mind made up. She's not moving."

They scheduled a C-section for September 7th—two days before the original due date. We were excited to have the date so that we could make a plan. It was also one week before opening day at the pumpkin patch.

Every year, we pick a theme for the pumpkin patch. We deck everything out with decorations, and I spray paint characters related to the theme on hay bales. That year, I picked the Disney movie, *Up*. In the first few minutes of the movie, one of the characters, Ellie, suffers a miscarriage. The movie hit so close to home after eight years of struggling with infertility and after losing Paislee. I was very passionate about the theme and what it meant to me. I worked hard to do the best job I could on the spray-painted bale characters and then we picked as many of the pumpkins as possible. We got everything prepared so that after the baby came, we would be able to be away for a few days and then rest at home until opening day.

On September 6th, we drove down to the hospital. The C-section was scheduled for 9:30 the next morning. My mom and brother came down to be with Mox at a hotel right across the street from the hospital; that way they could come visit us often. I don't think I got much sleep the night before—too much excitement and too many nerves. We were going to meet her very soon.

The next day, Cal and I went to the hospital at around 8:30 a.m. Mira was getting ready for the C-section and we went to her room. Jan was there with Mira's dad, Trey. They were so easy to talk to and such a friendly couple.

Everything was very calm in the room. I also had to get suited up and ready. Mira wanted Jan and me to be in the surgery room with her. She told me to go with the baby as soon as she was born. I was excited and thankful that Mira wanted me to be there and to be a part of that special moment; I was even allowed to bring my camera in. I was hoping I could capture the moment she came into the world.

It was almost time to go to the surgery room. The doctor came in and did one last ultrasound to confirm the baby's position before the surgery. Then it was time.

When we walked into the room, I couldn't believe how bright it was in there. Jan stayed very close to Mira and I stood back behind Jan. Once they got started, all I could think about was that we were all going to get to meet her so soon. I knew it would be such an amazing moment.

I felt Mira was being so strong. I can't imagine the feelings and pain she had to be experiencing. The doctor was working very fast and after a few minutes she pulled the baby out. Mira couldn't see, but she said, "She's here!"

I captured the first moment I saw her.

They took her over to weigh her and I got another picture. She was beautiful. She weighed exactly seven pounds. I know Mira wanted me to stay with the baby once she was born, but I also had to go over and make sure Mira was doing okay. I didn't want to leave either of them.

There were tears in my eyes as I went over to Mira. "Are you okay?"

She nodded, yes.

"She's beautiful," I told her, and she began to tear up too.

Then both she and Jan said, "Go. Go be with her."

MYA MAE

September 2018

O N SEPTEMBER 7TH, 2018 AT 9:36 A.M., Mya Mae was born.

The nurses took us to the room where Cal was waiting, and he got to meet her for the first time. I fed her her first bottle. Mira wanted us to spend some time with her on our own for a while, so we could bond with her, before she would meet her.

About fifteen minutes later, Mira was back in her recovery room. She asked the nurses if we could come over with Mya so she could meet her. When we got there, she looked like she was doing pretty well for having just had a C-section. She seemed to not be in any pain at all. I put Mya in her arms, and she shed some tears.

"She's so beautiful," Mira said.

Jan and Trey were also in the room. They got to hold Mya and then we all took a picture together. Mya was surrounded by so much love that day.

After about half an hour, they took us to the room where we would be staying for the rest of our time at the hospital. We were going to get some more time with Mya by ourselves and then we would go to Mira's room once she was settled in.

I was so excited for Mox to meet his sister. I called my mom right away. "Would you all like to come meet Mya?"

She, Mox, and Ray headed right on over. Mox was just about four years old at that time. I asked him if he would like to hold her for a bit. He said yes. I got a few pictures of them.

While Mox was holding her, Mya sneezed and started to cry.

"Mom?" Mox said.

"Yes?"

"Can you hold her now?"

We all smiled. I took Mya Mae in my arms and then he was off to explore the hospital room.

We visited Mira's room about three hours later. Joy also came up to make sure everything was going smoothly. She asked to hold Mya and when I handed her over, Mya started to cry right away. Joy handed her back to me and Mya stopped.

"She already knows you're Mom!" Joy said. It was hard to believe that Mya could already tell if I was the one holding her or not, but I felt like we bonded from the moment I first held her—and I guess she felt the same way.

I also was thinking of Mira at that moment. I hoped Joy's comment wasn't painful for her to hear. Or would she feel relieved to know that we had bonded so quickly, like she had wanted? It was hard for me to let myself be happy in those moments. I could never tell when my happiness might be causing pain for the birth family.

It wasn't long before Mira started to be in a lot of pain. We stayed and visited for just a little bit and then we left to let her rest. After we got back to our room, Mox, Mom, and Ray came back and brought us supper. I was incredibly hungry. I don't think I had eaten since before Mya was born. Ray got me a cheeseburger and I'm pretty sure it was the best burger I've ever eaten.

They stayed until it was bedtime for Mox and then headed back to the hotel. It was so nice to have them so close. Mox said he could look out the window and see the "Hossiple." We stayed at the hospital for the next two days and spent most of our time in Mira's room so she could spend all the time she wanted with Mya. On September 9th, a photographer came to the room to take some pictures of Mya and Mira together, and some of Cal and me with her.

One of the first things the photographer said was, "I want to make sure I don't say the wrong words here, so how would you all like to be addressed?"

Mira looked at Cal and me right away and said, "They're Mom and Dad."

It was only a little bit after the session when the photographer came back to show us the photos. We were all looking at them and Mira began to cry. She headed to the bathroom to be alone. Joy, Jan, and Trey were in the room at the time so they could all be there for her. She didn't have to go through this alone.

On the night of the 9th they told us that we were all going to be discharged the next morning around noon. We were very excited to get to go home. We had been in the hospital for three days.

In the morning, Jan came to be with Mira before we were discharged. Trey had said his goodbyes the night before—he said it would be too hard to be there when we were leaving; Joy came on the last day to be with everyone and to make sure all the final paperwork was signed. She had us all leave the room so Mira could have a few minutes with Mya by herself to say goodbye.

Mira decided that she wanted us all to walk out of the hospital together, so we got Mya strapped in her car seat, which we did with confidence this time.

We took our final pictures all together and started on the very long walk to the main entrance. I felt like it took twenty minutes to get outside. I think I was so excited to see Mox and be out in the sunlight. Once we got there, Mom, Ray, and Mox were all waiting for us right beside our car.

"Mox, are you ready to go home with Mya?" I said.

"Yep!" In a couple of seconds, he was strapped into his car seat.

It was time. Again.

We all gave each other hugs and said our goodbyes. While I was hugging Mira, I started to cry. I told her to take care and let her know how much Mya was already loved. It's so hard to know what to say in those moments. I don't know if the words helped, but I hoped they would.

My mom and Ray stood back a bit as we all said our goodbyes. They were crying too, as they watched it all unfold. They said it was so emotional to watch. After knowing what happened the first time with Kip, it was also a relief to actually be leaving the hospital. They were so happy for us, but they also saw the other side of it as Mira said goodbye to Mya.

Adoption is such a weight on everyone's emotions. It brings people together and makes families whole; but, at the same time, it tears people's hearts in two.

I gave Mom and Ray hugs and thanked them for being there and being with Mox while we were at the hospital. I so appreciated knowing he was close by and having a good time with them. I appreciated it more than they could know.

We all got in the car and I sat in the back with Mox and Mya. As we drove out of the front driveway of the hospital, I looked back and waved at everyone who'd come to see us off. The emotions that filled me in that moment were overwhelming. There was grief and pain mixed with so much joy and thankfulness. My eyes blurred with tears and I held my babies close.

We were driving off to start our life as a family of four again. And on September 13th, three days after we got home, Mira went to her court hearing and it was official: Mya Mae was here to stay.

AFTERWORD

WHEN WE WERE FIRST GOING THROUGH OUR struggle with infertility and trying so hard to get pregnant, I was always thinking of our losses. I wanted to look at our children and see us in them. In the end, that did happen—just not in the way I thought it would.

They are part of us. They are the journey we went on to bring them into our lives. Cal and I went through the whole process together, side by side, and when we look at them, we see that. I don't ever see that as a loss.

Mox is the sweetest, soft-hearted, kind boy. Mya is our tiny princess with a big personality. I love them so very much. They're both my rainbows. They're both our dreams come true. I didn't give birth to them, but I couldn't love them any more even if I had.

The love for each of our four children was instant from the moment we met them. They may not all be with us today, but they will always hold a place in our hearts. We had to fight for them. We had to keep hoping and praying for them. God knew I was going to be a mom. He put the fight in me to bring them into my life. Our journey wasn't easy, and it didn't go the way we planned, but I can't imagine our life any other way.

To anyone out there struggling with infertility or waiting for The Call: I see you. Never lose hope. There may be a bigger plan in the works. Never stop fighting for your dream and keep putting one foot in front of the other. Somewhere at the end of that road, you will find your rainbow.

In memory of

Paislee Rae

ACKNOWLEDGMENTS

THERE ARE SO MANY PEOPLE THAT PLAY A PART in the making of a book. There are those who touch the actual manuscript, of course, but then there are those who affect the creation of the story itself.

To my husband Cal, thank you for never leaving my side through all of this. We went on a roller-coaster ride that we weren't expecting. We went into every high and low together and came out of all of them together. I'm so thankful that we had each other every step of the way.

To all the birth mothers and fathers who made us the Berry family, thank you. We would not be who we are today without you, and this book might never have happened. Faye, Hannah and Derek, and

Mira—you all gave me the gift of being a mother and I will never forget that. I will never stop being grateful to you.

To our family, friends, and The Village Family Service Center, you were there for us on our journey every step of the way. You were the encouraging voices that helped us keep going. Thank you so much for your love and support.

Finally, a huge thanks goes out to the people who put *Waiting for Rainbows* together: TSPA The Self Publishing Agency team. I am so grateful to Megan for her encouragement and boundless support, to Anna for her thoughtful questions and guidance, and to Elise for her ability to turn a few notes into a paragraph that describes exactly how I was feeling. She truly made our story come to life and working with her was such an amazing experience. I also want to thank Alison for her editorial eye and the feedback she provided along the way, Stephanie and Kristy for their exceptional design skills, Ira for all the work she did behind the scenes to keep the project on track, and Jennica Maes, my first beta reader!

Thank you all so much for your guidance and support along the way and for helping put *Waiting for Rainbows* in my hands!

ASHLEY BERRY lives in North Dakota with her husband and their two adopted children. They operate a family-run greenhouse, and every fall they have a pumpkin patch and a corn maze. Ashley also has a degree in photography and enjoys capturing birth stories in her spare time. She has seen firsthand the devastating effects of infertility for couples and individuals alike and hopes her story will encourage and remind her readers to keep striving and living in hope as they wait for their rainbow.